W9-CBT-507

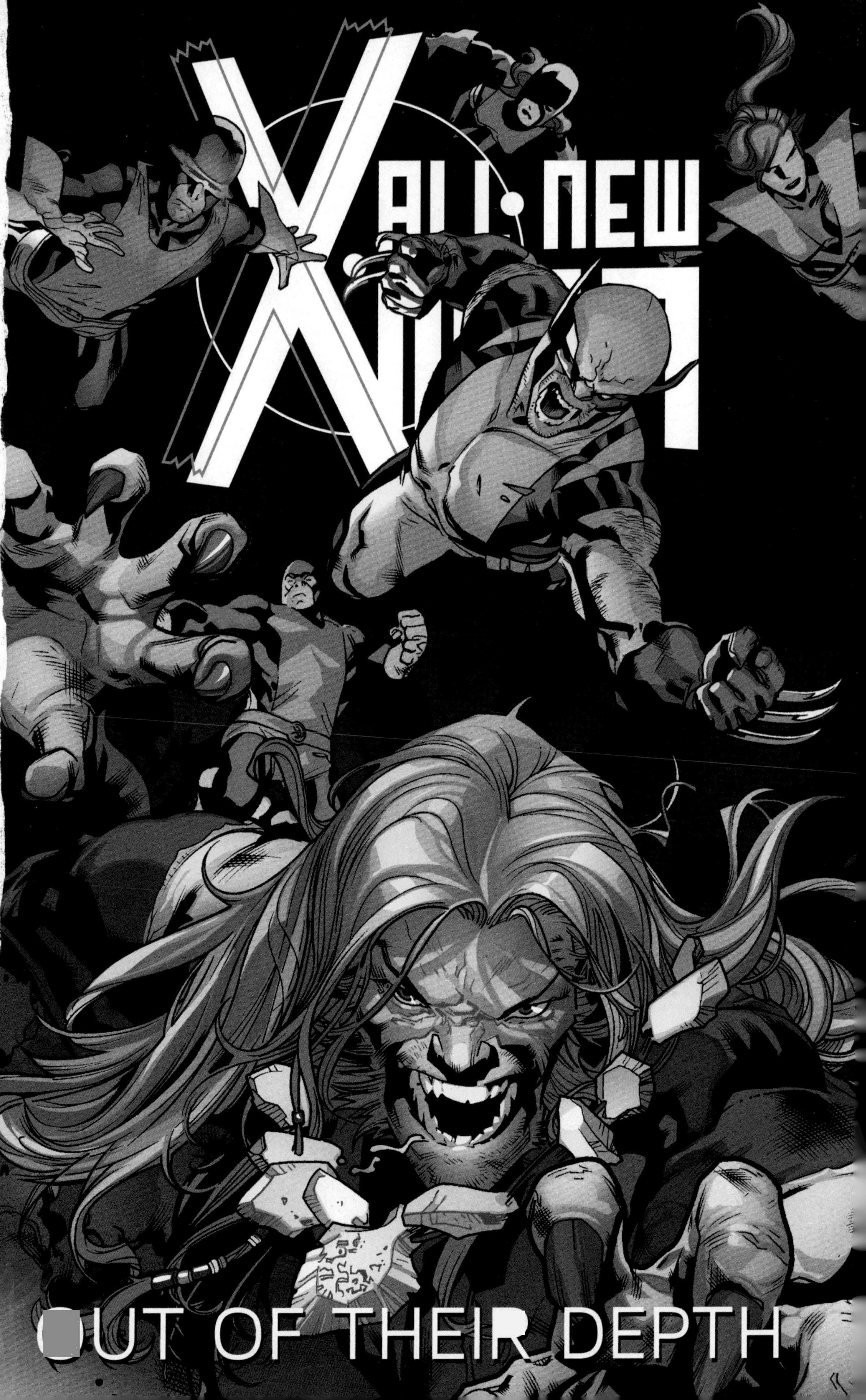
ALL-NEW X
OUT OF THEIR DEPTH

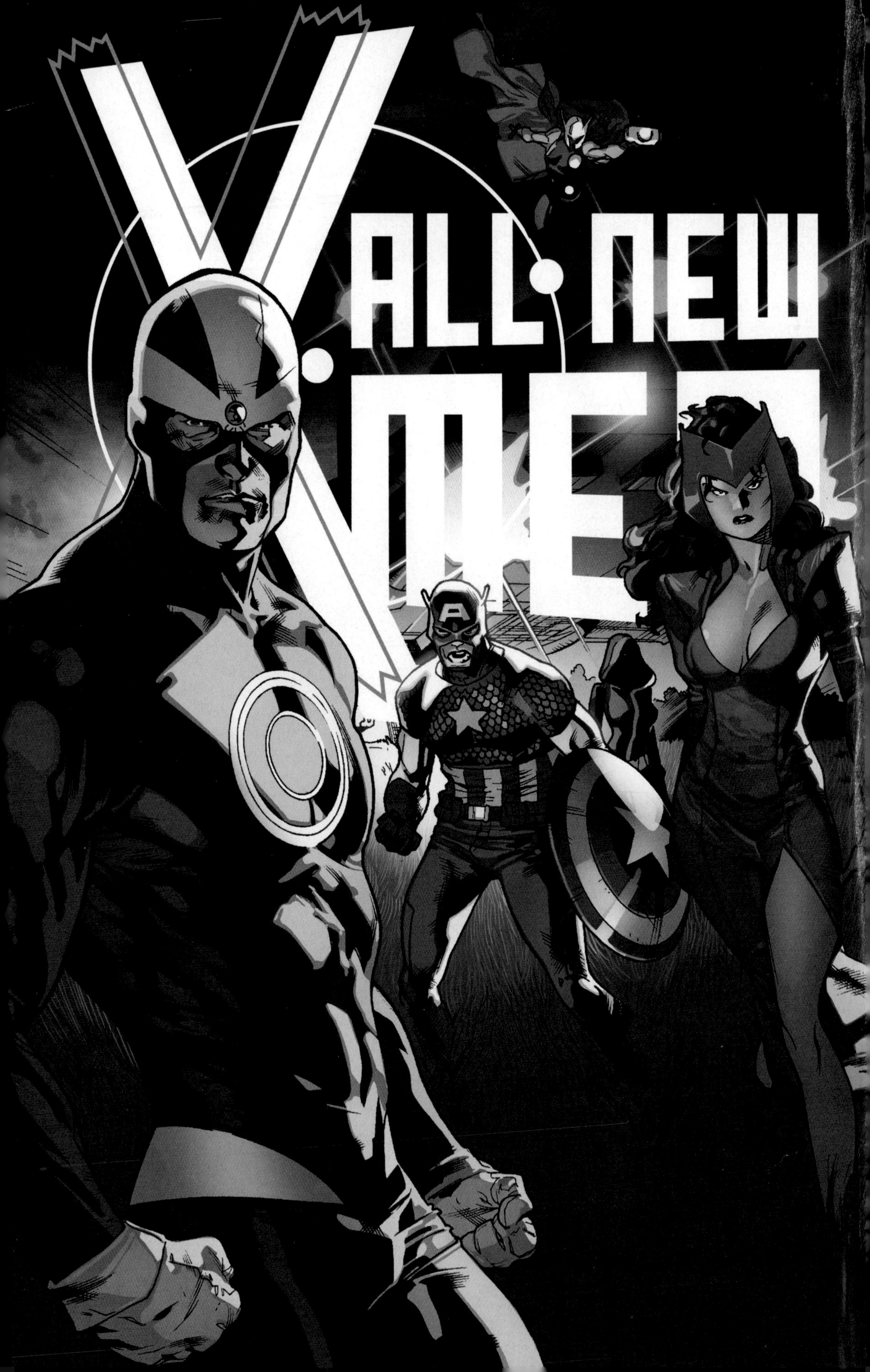
ALL-NEW
X-MEN

BEAST
HANK McCOY

MARVEL GIRL
JEAN GREY

CYCLOPS
SCOTT SUMMERS

ANGEL
WARREN WORTHINGTON III

ICEMAN
BOBBY DRAKE

OUT OF THEIR DEPTH

BRIAN MICHAEL
BENDIS
WRITER

STUART
IMMONEN
PENCILER, #11-14

WADE VON
GRAWBADGER
INKER, #11-14

DAVID
LAFUENTE
ARTIST, #15

MARTE
GRACIA
COLORIST, #11 & #14

RAIN
BEREDO
COLORIST, #12-13

JAMES
CAMPBELL
COLORIST, #15

COVER ART: **STUART IMMONEN, WADE VON GRAWBADGER & MARTE GRACIA** WITH RAIN BEREDO (COLORS, #15)

VC'S CORY
PETIT
LETTERER

JORDAN D.
WHITE
ASSISTANT EDITOR

NICK
LOWE
EDITOR

COLLECTION EDITOR: **JENNIFER GRÜNWALD**
ASSISTANT EDITORS: **ALEX STARBUCK** & **NELSON RIBEIRO**
EDITOR, SPECIAL PROJECTS: **MARK D. BEAZLEY**
SENIOR EDITOR, SPECIAL PROJECTS: **JEFF YOUNGQUIST**
SVP OF PRINT & DIGITAL PUBLISHING SALES: **DAVID GABRIEL**
BOOK DESIGNER: **RODOLFO MURAGUCHI**

EDITOR IN CHIEF: **AXEL ALONSO**
CHIEF CREATIVE OFFICER: **JOE QUESADA**
PUBLISHER: **DAN BUCKLEY**
EXECUTIVE PRODUCER: **ALAN FINE**

ALL-NEW X-MEN VOL. 3: OUT OF THEIR DEPTH. Contains material originally published in magazine form as ALL-NEW X-MEN 11-15. First printing 2013. ISBN# 978-0-7851-6822-5. Published by MARVEL WORLDWIDE, INC., a subsidiary of MARVEL ENTERTAINMENT, LLC. OFFICE OF PUBLICATION: 135 West 50th Street, New York, NY 10020. Copyright © 2013 Marvel Characters, Inc. All rights reserved. All characters featured in this issue and the distinctive names and likenesses thereof, and all related indicia are trademarks of Marvel Characters, Inc. No similarity between any of the names, characters, persons, and/or institutions in this magazine with those of any living or dead person or institution is intended, and any such similarity which may exist is purely coincidental. **Printed in the U.S.A.** ALAN FINE, EVP - Office of the President, Marvel Worldwide, Inc. and EVP & CMO Marvel Characters B.V.; DAN BUCKLEY, Publisher & President - Print, Animation & Digital Divisions; JOE QUESADA, Chief Creative Officer; TOM BREVOORT, SVP of Publishing; DAVID BOGART, SVP of Operations & Procurement, Publishing; C.B. CEBULSKI, SVP of Creator & Content Development; DAVID GABRIEL, SVP of Print & Digital Publishing Sales; JIM O'KEEFE, VP of Operations & Logistics; DAN CARR, Executive Director of Publishing Technology; SUSAN CRESPI, Editorial Operations Manager; ALEX MORALES, Publishing Operations Manager; STAN LEE, Chairman Emeritus. For information regarding advertising in Marvel Comics or on Marvel.com, please contact Niza Disla, Director of Marvel Partnerships, at ndisla@marvel.com. For Marvel subscription inquiries, please call 800-217-

Born with genetic mutations that gave them abilities beyond those of normal humans, mutants are the next stage in evolution. As such, they are feared and hated by humanity. A group of mutants known as the X-Men fight for peaceful coexistence between mutants and humankind. But not all mutants see peaceful coextistence as a reality.

X·ALL·NEW
X·MEN

The original X-Men — Cyclops, Angel, Iceman, Beast and Marvel Girl — have travelled from past to present and, after learning of the tragedies awaiting them, voted to stay. They want to help realize Xavier's dream before their destinies get in the way, but it might be too late for Jean Grey, who's been prematurely burdened by her psychic powers and adult memories.

Meanwhile, the shape-shifting mutant known as Mystique recruited Sabretooth and Mastermind to take the humans for everything they can. Posing as X-Men during robberies, they're driving the wedge between mutants and humans even deeper.

Modern-day Cyclops is more interested in mutant prosperity than mutant-human relations. His mission to bring new mutants to his Xavier school took him all over the world, and finally to the Jean Grey School.

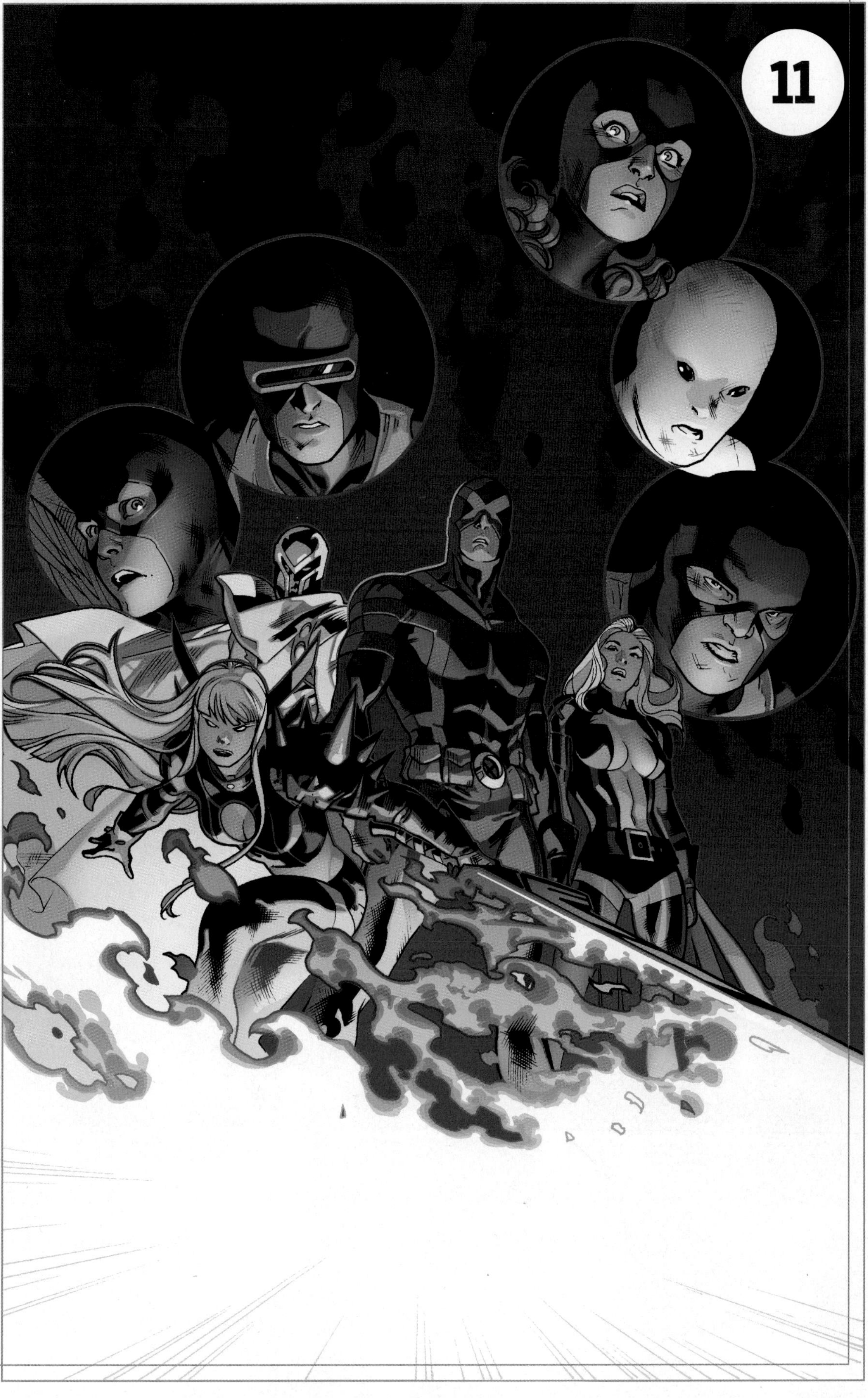
11

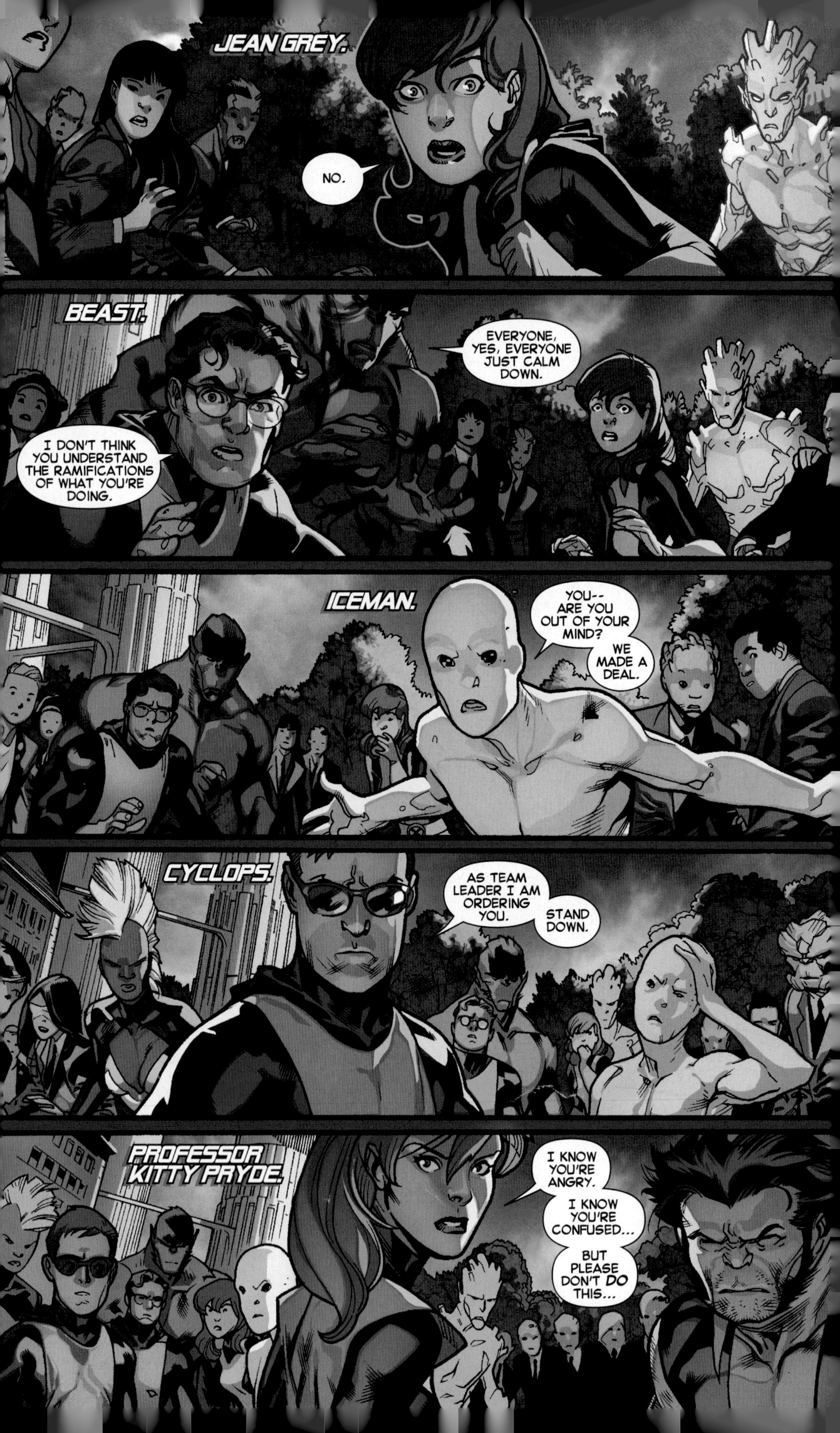
JEAN GREY.
NO.
BEAST.
EVERYONE, YES, EVERYONE JUST CALM DOWN.
I DON'T THINK YOU UNDERSTAND THE RAMIFICATIONS OF WHAT YOU'RE DOING.
ICEMAN.
YOU-- ARE YOU OUT OF YOUR MIND?
WE MADE A DEAL.
CYCLOPS.
AS TEAM LEADER I AM ORDERING YOU.
STAND DOWN.
PROFESSOR KITTY PRYDE.
I KNOW YOU'RE ANGRY.
I KNOW YOU'RE CONFUSED...
BUT PLEASE DON'T DO THIS...

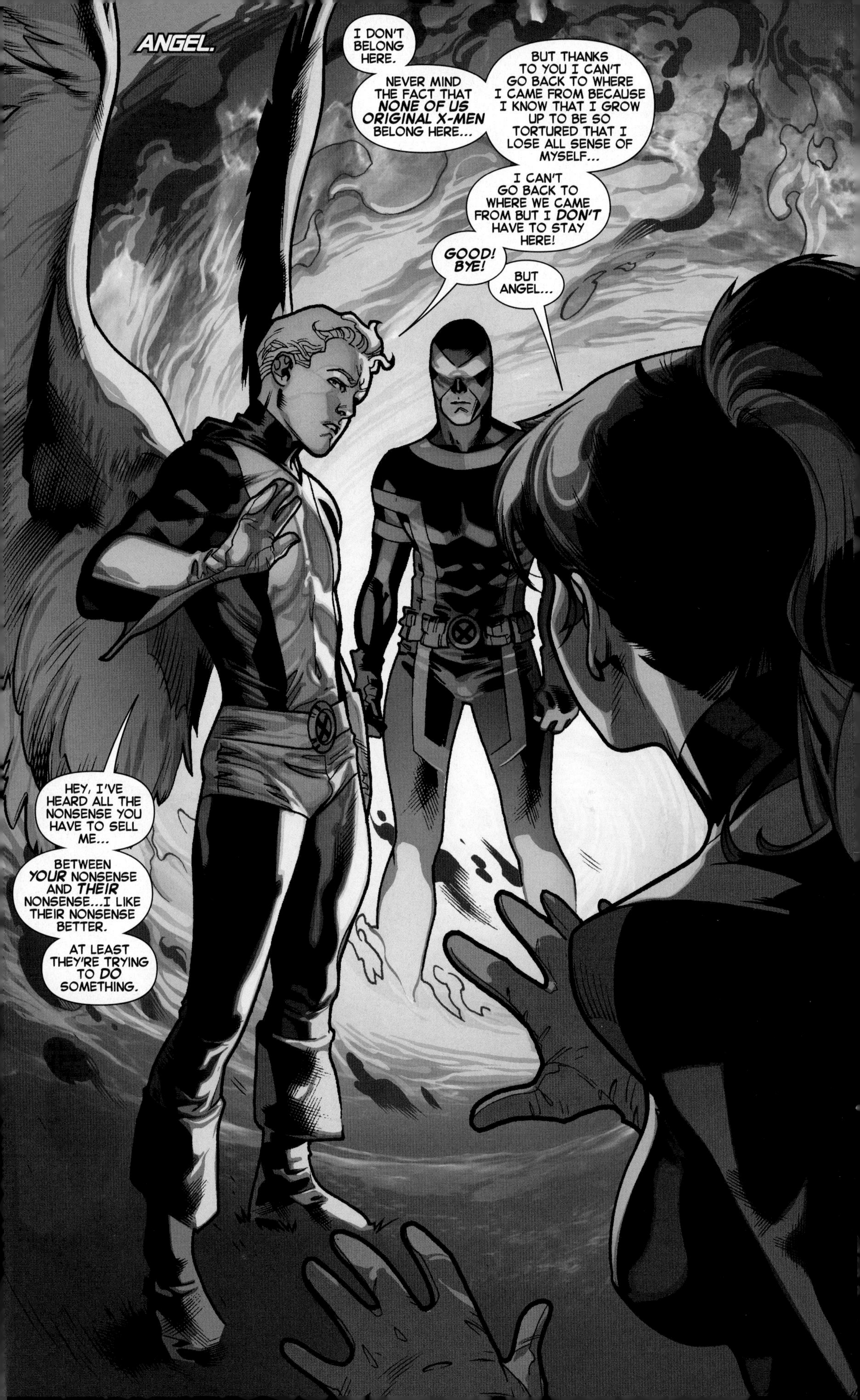
ANGEL.
I DON'T BELONG HERE.
NEVER MIND THE FACT THAT NONE OF US ORIGINAL X-MEN BELONG HERE...
BUT THANKS TO YOU I CAN'T GO BACK TO WHERE I CAME FROM BECAUSE I KNOW THAT I GROW UP TO BE SO TORTURED THAT I LOSE ALL SENSE OF MYSELF...
I CAN'T GO BACK TO WHERE WE CAME FROM BUT I DON'T HAVE TO STAY HERE!
GOOD! BYE!
BUT ANGEL...
HEY, I'VE HEARD ALL THE NONSENSE YOU HAVE TO SELL ME...
BETWEEN YOUR NONSENSE AND THEIR NONSENSE...I LIKE THEIR NONSENSE BETTER.
AT LEAST THEY'RE TRYING TO DO SOMETHING.

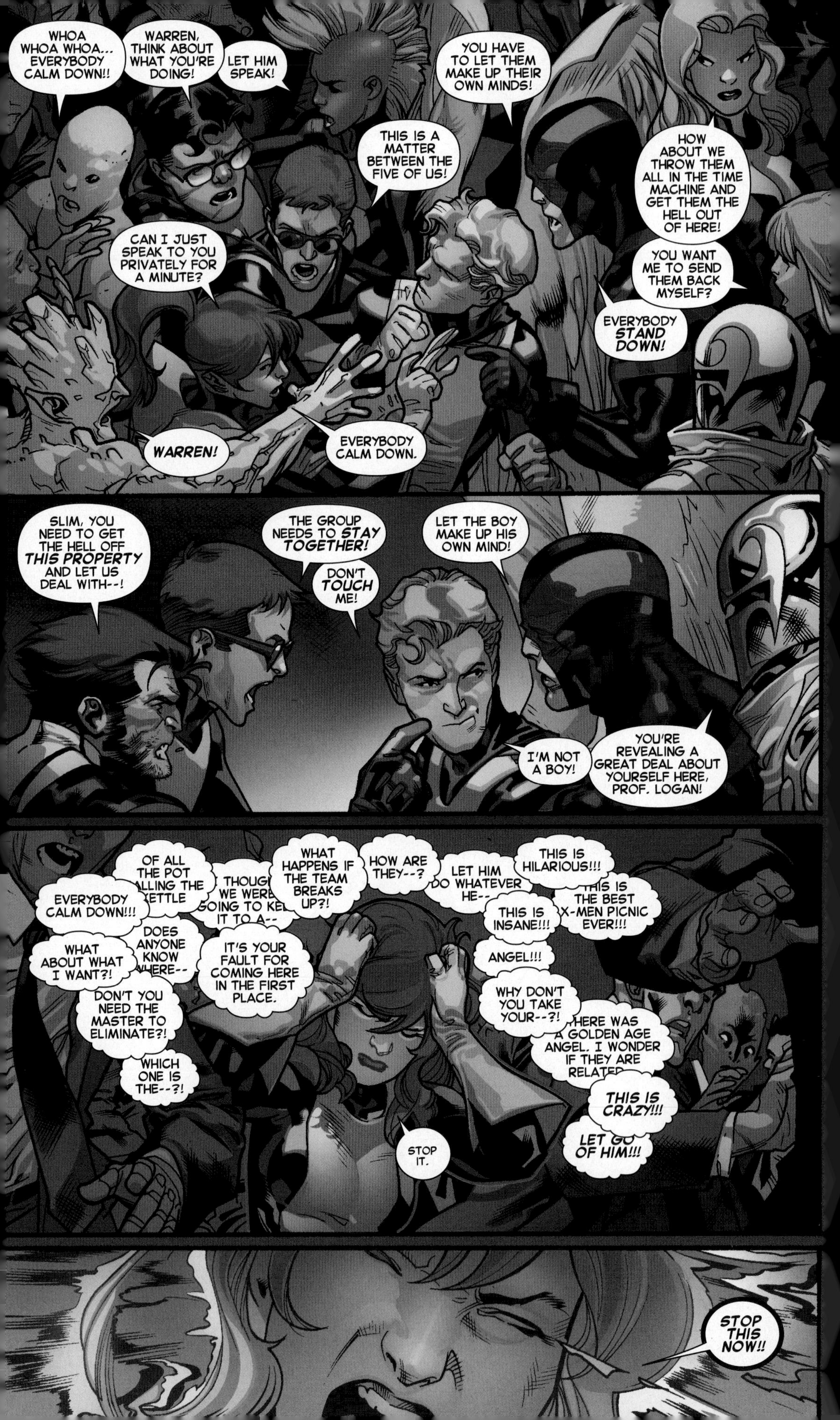
WHOA WHOA WHOA... EVERYBODY CALM DOWN!!
WARREN, THINK ABOUT WHAT YOU'RE DOING!
LET HIM SPEAK!
YOU HAVE TO LET THEM MAKE UP THEIR OWN MINDS!
THIS IS A MATTER BETWEEN THE FIVE OF US!
HOW ABOUT WE THROW THEM ALL IN THE TIME MACHINE AND GET THEM THE HELL OUT OF HERE!
CAN I JUST SPEAK TO YOU PRIVATELY FOR A MINUTE?
YOU WANT ME TO SEND THEM BACK MYSELF?
EVERYBODY STAND DOWN!
WARREN!
EVERYBODY CALM DOWN.
SLIM, YOU NEED TO GET THE HELL OFF THIS PROPERTY AND LET US DEAL WITH--!
THE GROUP NEEDS TO STAY TOGETHER!
DON'T TOUCH ME!
LET THE BOY MAKE UP HIS OWN MIND!
I'M NOT A BOY!
YOU'RE REVEALING A GREAT DEAL ABOUT YOURSELF HERE, PROF. LOGAN!
EVERYBODY CALM DOWN!!!
OF ALL THE POT ALLING THE ETTLE
THOUG WE WERE OING TO KE IT TO A--
WHAT HAPPENS IF THE TEAM BREAKS UP?!
HOW ARE THEY--?
LET HIM DO WHATEVER HE--
THIS IS HILARIOUS!!!
THIS IS THE BEST X-MEN PICNIC EVER!!!
THIS IS INSANE!!!
WHAT ABOUT WHAT I WANT?!
DOES ANYONE KNOW WHERE--
IT'S YOUR FAULT FOR COMING HERE IN THE FIRST PLACE.
ANGEL!!!
DON'T YOU NEED THE MASTER TO ELIMINATE?!
WHY DON'T YOU TAKE YOUR--?!
HERE WAS A GOLDEN AGE ANGEL. I WONDER IF THEY ARE RELATE
WHICH ONE IS THE--?!
THIS IS CRAZY!!!
LET GO OF HIM!!!
STOP IT.
STOP THIS NOW!!

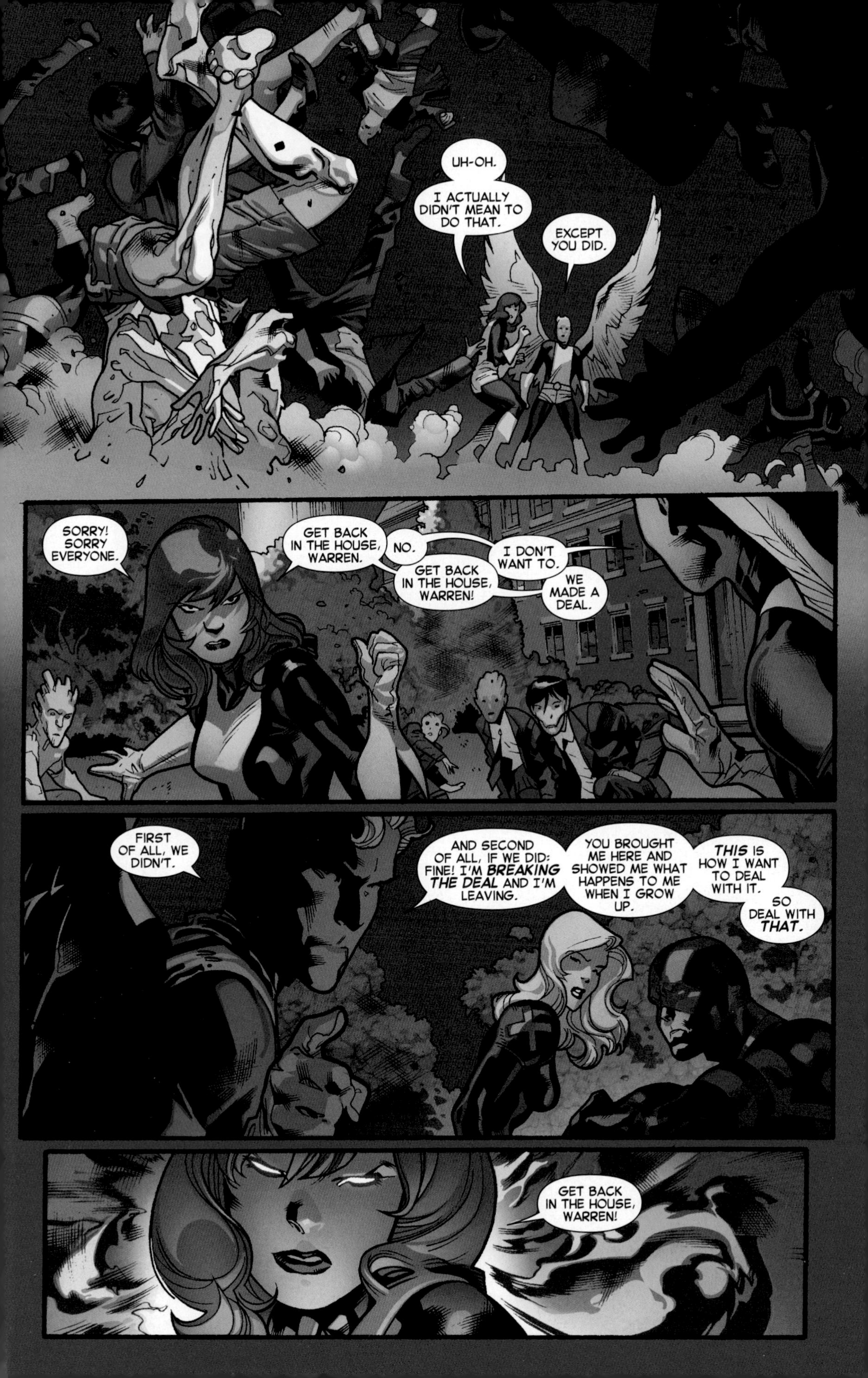
UH-OH.
I ACTUALLY DIDN'T MEAN TO DO THAT.
EXCEPT YOU DID.
SORRY! SORRY EVERYONE.
GET BACK IN THE HOUSE, WARREN.
NO.
I DON'T WANT TO.
GET BACK IN THE HOUSE, WARREN!
WE MADE A DEAL.
FIRST OF ALL, WE DIDN'T.
AND SECOND OF ALL, IF WE DID: FINE! I'M BREAKING THE DEAL AND I'M LEAVING.
YOU BROUGHT ME HERE AND SHOWED ME WHAT HAPPENS TO ME WHEN I GROW UP.
THIS IS HOW I WANT TO DEAL WITH IT.
SO DEAL WITH THAT.
GET BACK IN THE HOUSE, WARREN!

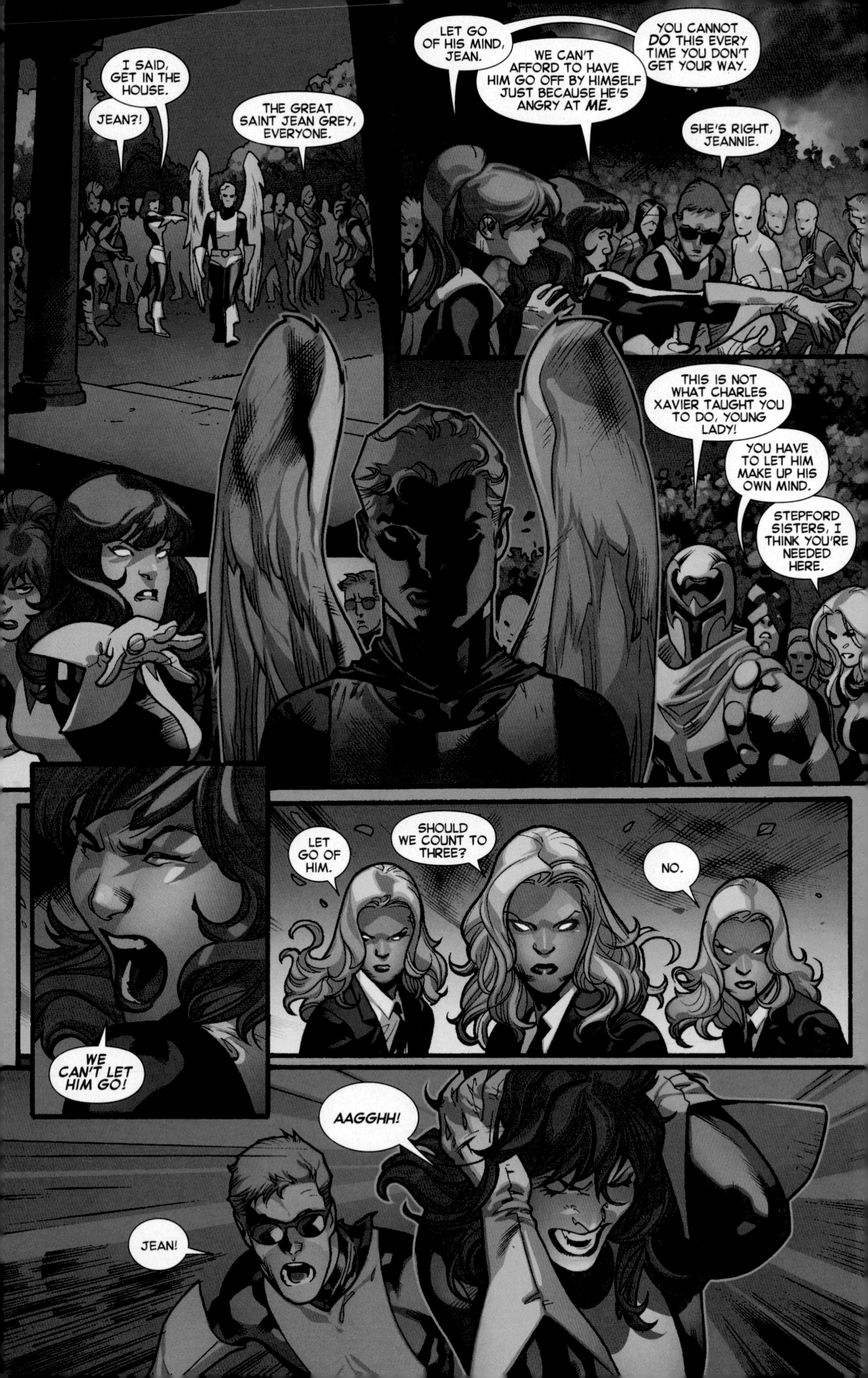
I SAID, GET IN THE HOUSE.
JEAN?!
THE GREAT SAINT JEAN GREY, EVERYONE.
LET GO OF HIS MIND, JEAN.
YOU CANNOT DO THIS EVERY TIME YOU DON'T GET YOUR WAY.
WE CAN'T AFFORD TO HAVE HIM GO OFF BY HIMSELF JUST BECAUSE HE'S ANGRY AT ME.
SHE'S RIGHT, JEANNIE.
THIS IS NOT WHAT CHARLES XAVIER TAUGHT YOU TO DO, YOUNG LADY!
YOU HAVE TO LET HIM MAKE UP HIS OWN MIND.
STEPFORD SISTERS, I THINK YOU'RE NEEDED HERE.
WE CAN'T LET HIM GO!
LET GO OF HIM.
SHOULD WE COUNT TO THREE?
NO.
AAGGHH!
JEAN!

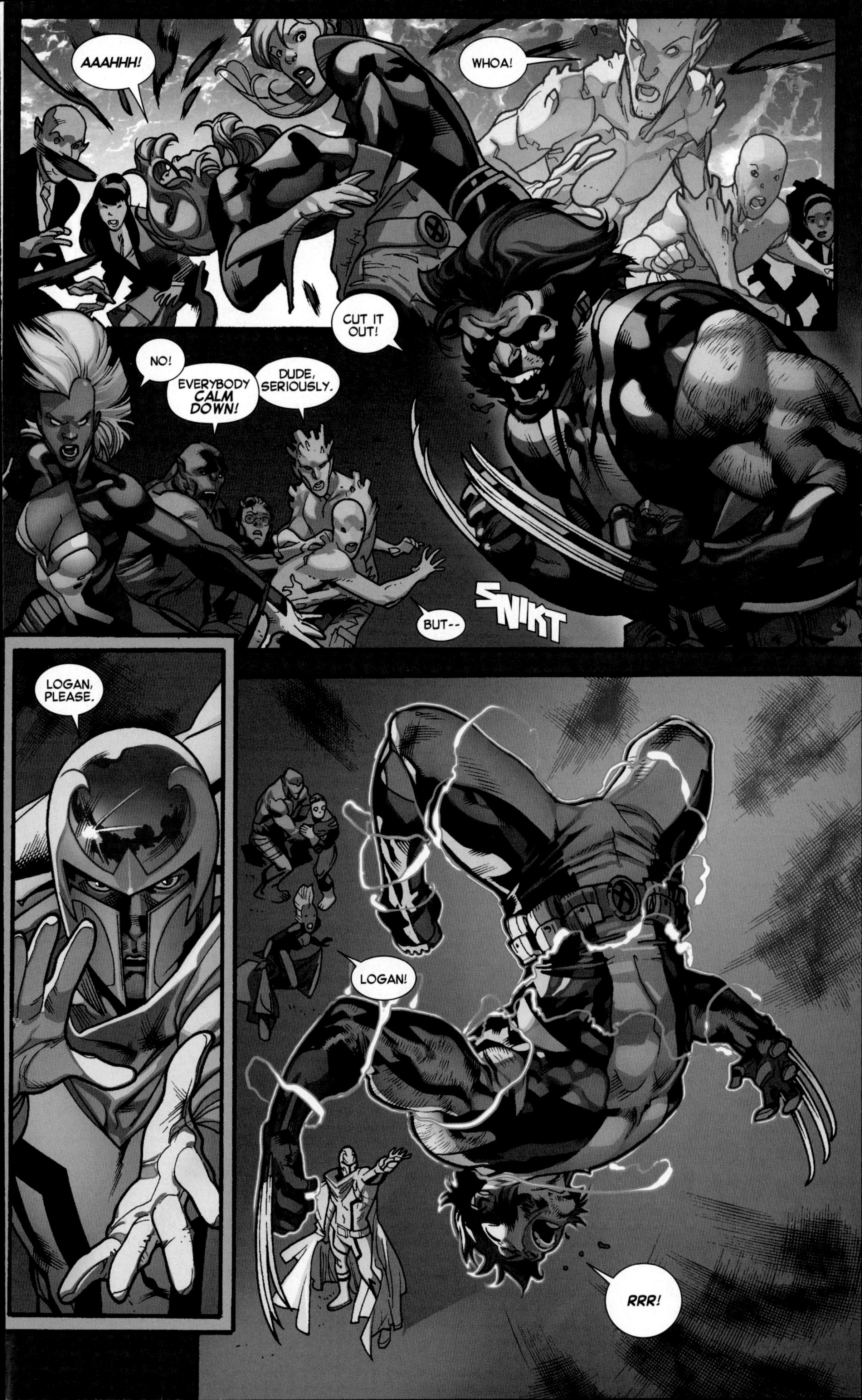
AAAHHH!
WHOA!
CUT IT OUT!
NO!
EVERYBODY CALM DOWN!
DUDE, SERIOUSLY.
BUT--
SNIKT
LOGAN, PLEASE.
LOGAN!
RRR!

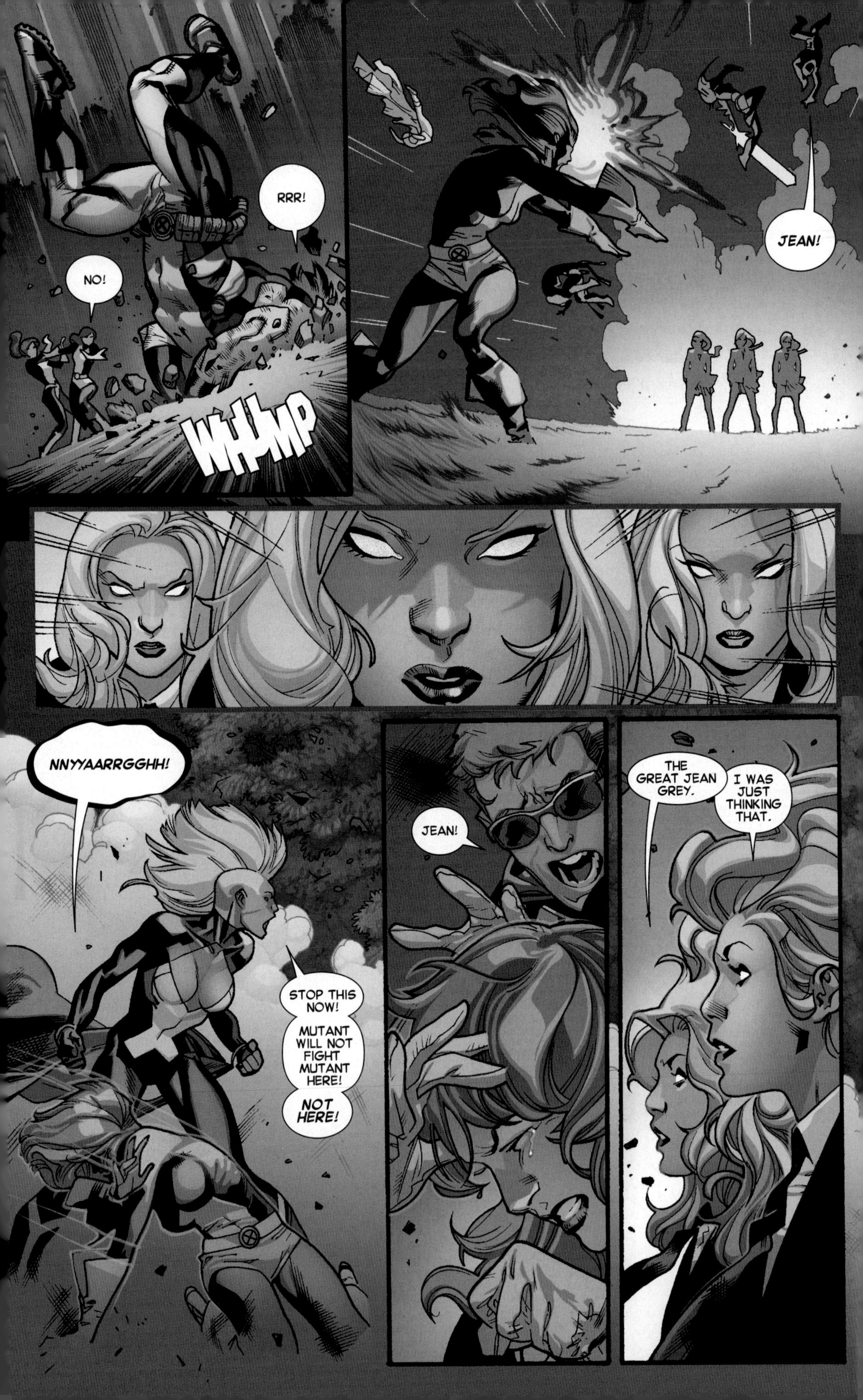
RRR!
NO!
WHUMP
JEAN!
NNYYAARRGGHH!
STOP THIS NOW!
MUTANT WILL NOT FIGHT MUTANT HERE!
NOT HERE!
JEAN!
THE GREAT JEAN GREY.
I WAS JUST THINKING THAT.

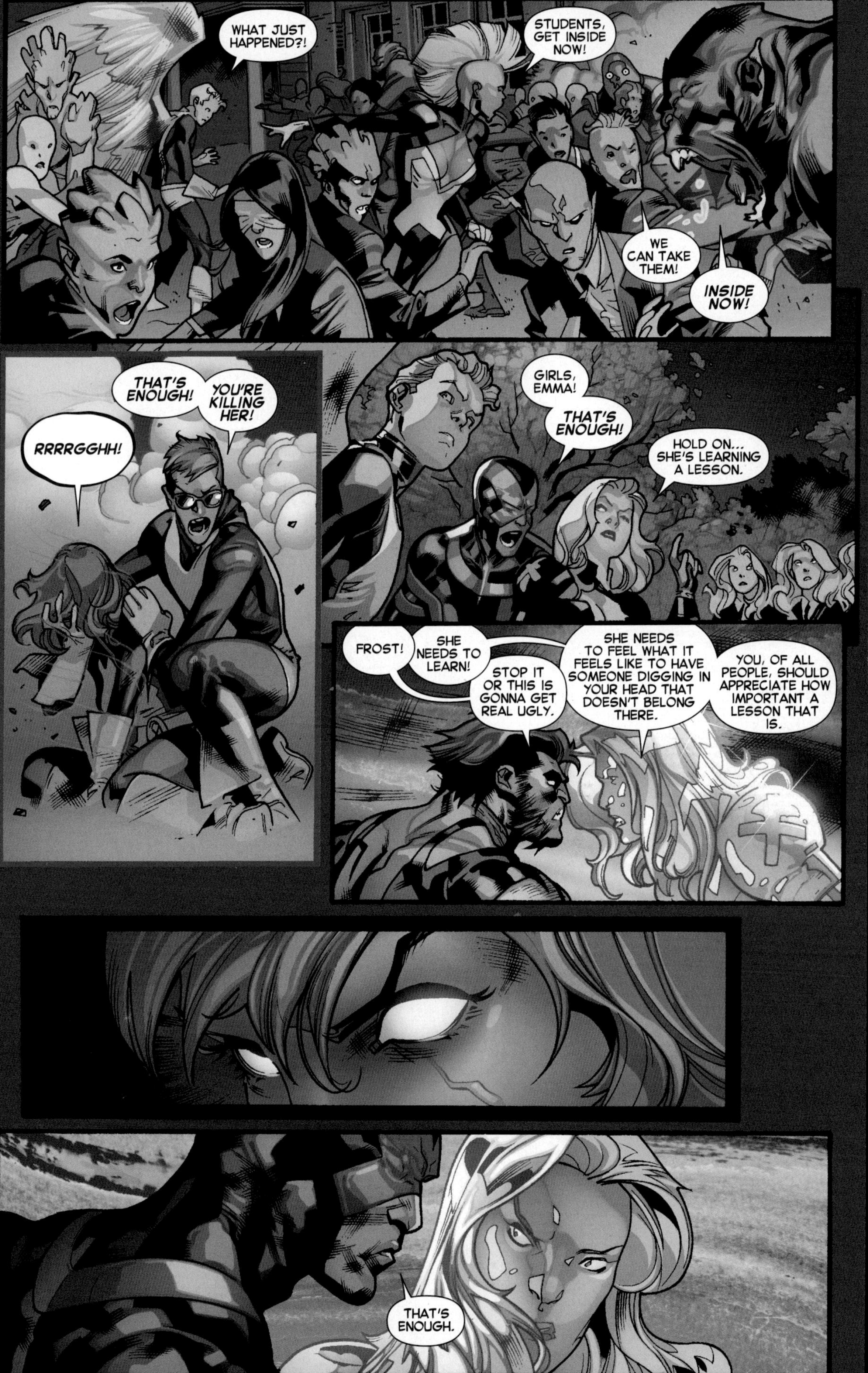
WHAT JUST HAPPENED?!
STUDENTS, GET INSIDE NOW!
WE CAN TAKE THEM!
INSIDE NOW!
THAT'S ENOUGH!
YOU'RE KILLING HER!
RRRRGGHH!
GIRLS, EMMA!
THAT'S ENOUGH!
HOLD ON... SHE'S LEARNING A LESSON.
FROST!
SHE NEEDS TO LEARN!
STOP IT OR THIS IS GONNA GET REAL UGLY.
SHE NEEDS TO FEEL WHAT IT FEELS LIKE TO HAVE SOMEONE DIGGING IN YOUR HEAD THAT DOESN'T BELONG THERE.
YOU, OF ALL PEOPLE, SHOULD APPRECIATE HOW IMPORTANT A LESSON THAT IS.
THAT'S ENOUGH.

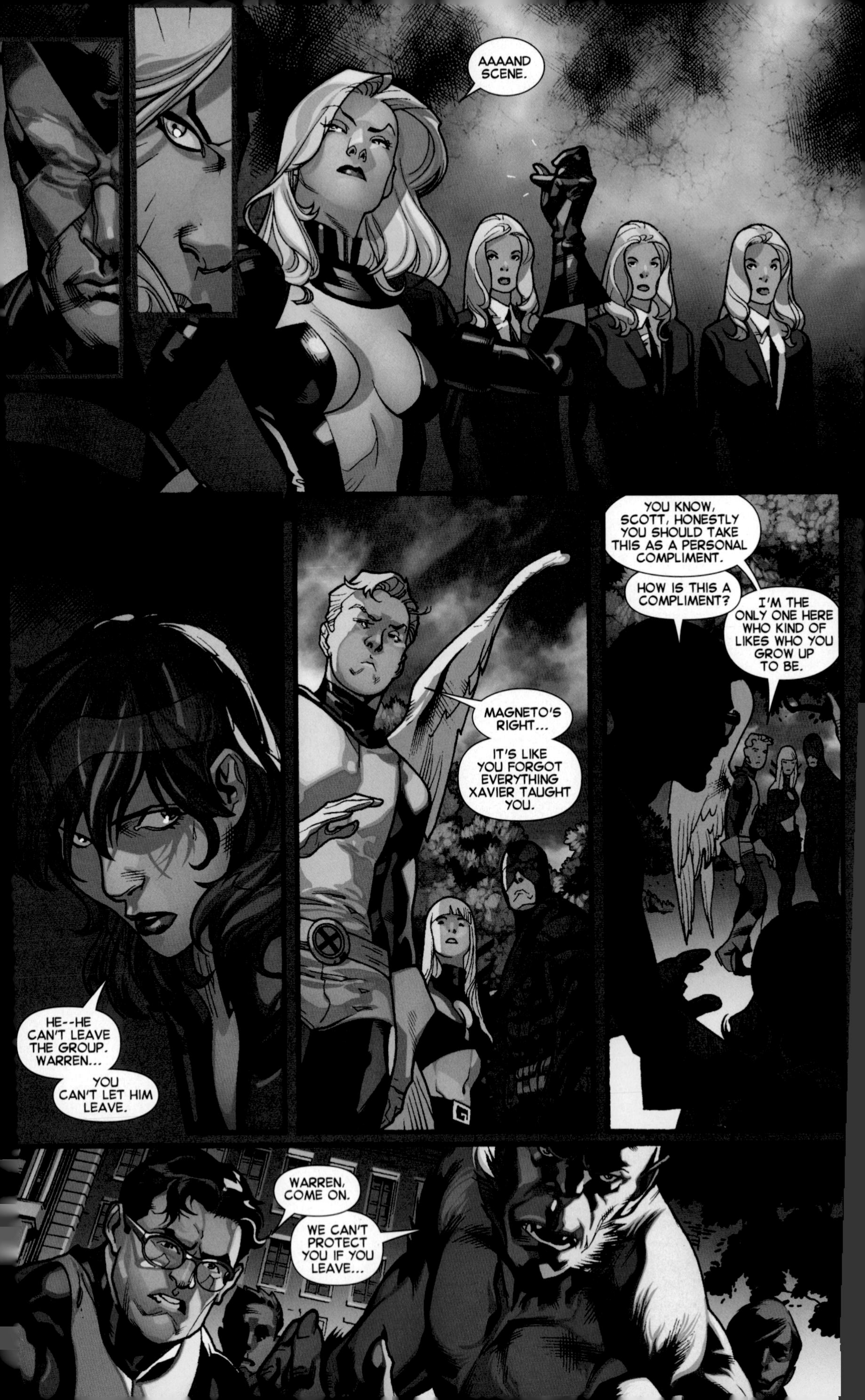
AAAAND SCENE.
HE--HE CAN'T LEAVE THE GROUP. WARREN...
YOU CAN'T LET HIM LEAVE.
MAGNETO'S RIGHT...
IT'S LIKE YOU FORGOT EVERYTHING XAVIER TAUGHT YOU.
YOU KNOW, SCOTT, HONESTLY YOU SHOULD TAKE THIS AS A PERSONAL COMPLIMENT.
HOW IS THIS A COMPLIMENT?
I'M THE ONLY ONE HERE WHO KIND OF LIKES WHO YOU GROW UP TO BE.
WARREN, COME ON.
WE CAN'T PROTECT YOU IF YOU LEAVE...

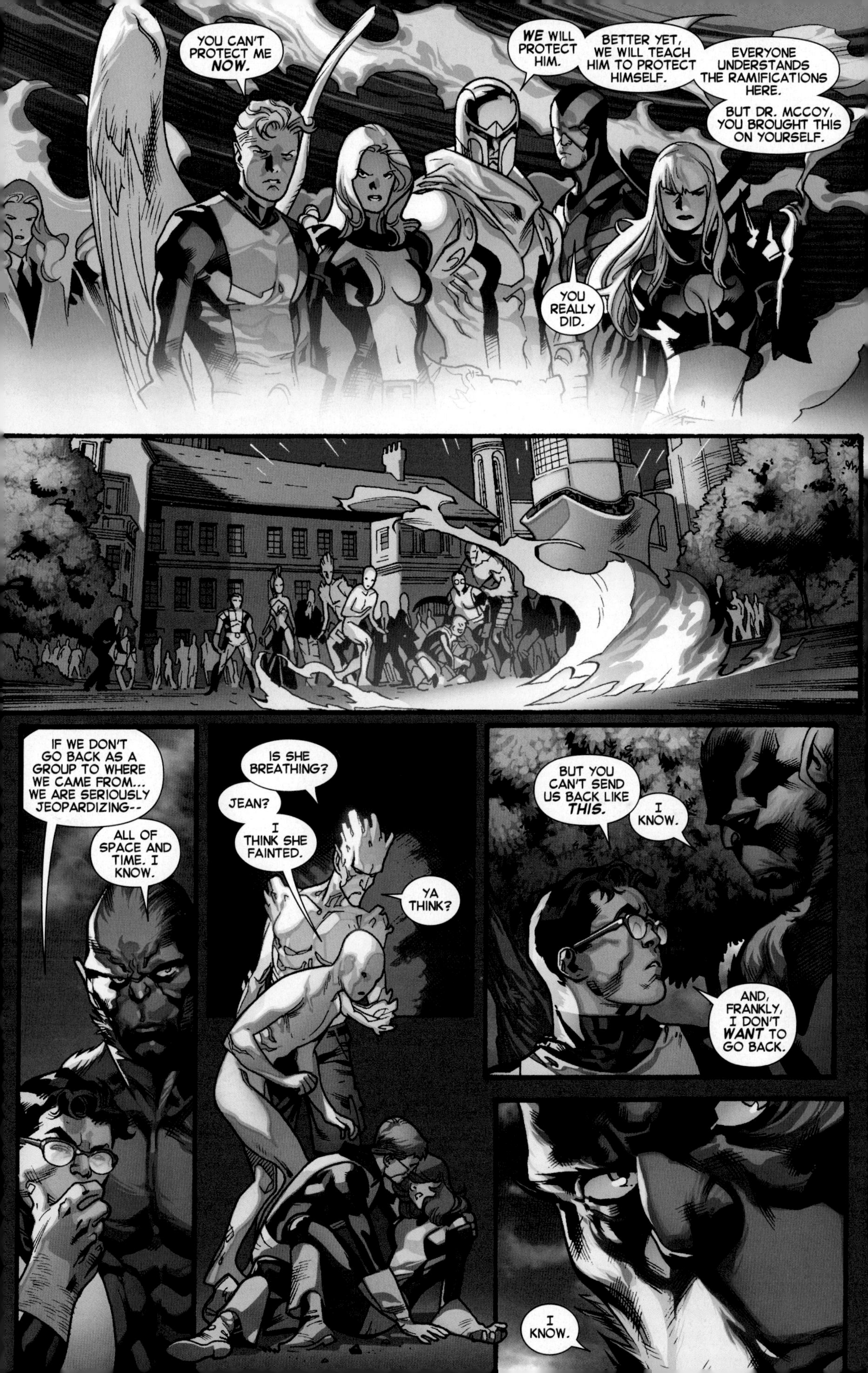
YOU CAN'T PROTECT ME NOW.
WE WILL PROTECT HIM.
BETTER YET, WE WILL TEACH HIM TO PROTECT HIMSELF.
EVERYONE UNDERSTANDS THE RAMIFICATIONS HERE.
BUT DR. MCCOY, YOU BROUGHT THIS ON YOURSELF.
YOU REALLY DID.
IF WE DON'T GO BACK AS A GROUP TO WHERE WE CAME FROM... WE ARE SERIOUSLY JEOPARDIZING--
ALL OF SPACE AND TIME. I KNOW.
IS SHE BREATHING?
JEAN?
I THINK SHE FAINTED.
YA THINK?
BUT YOU CAN'T SEND US BACK LIKE THIS.
I KNOW.
AND, FRANKLY, I DON'T WANT TO GO BACK.
I KNOW.

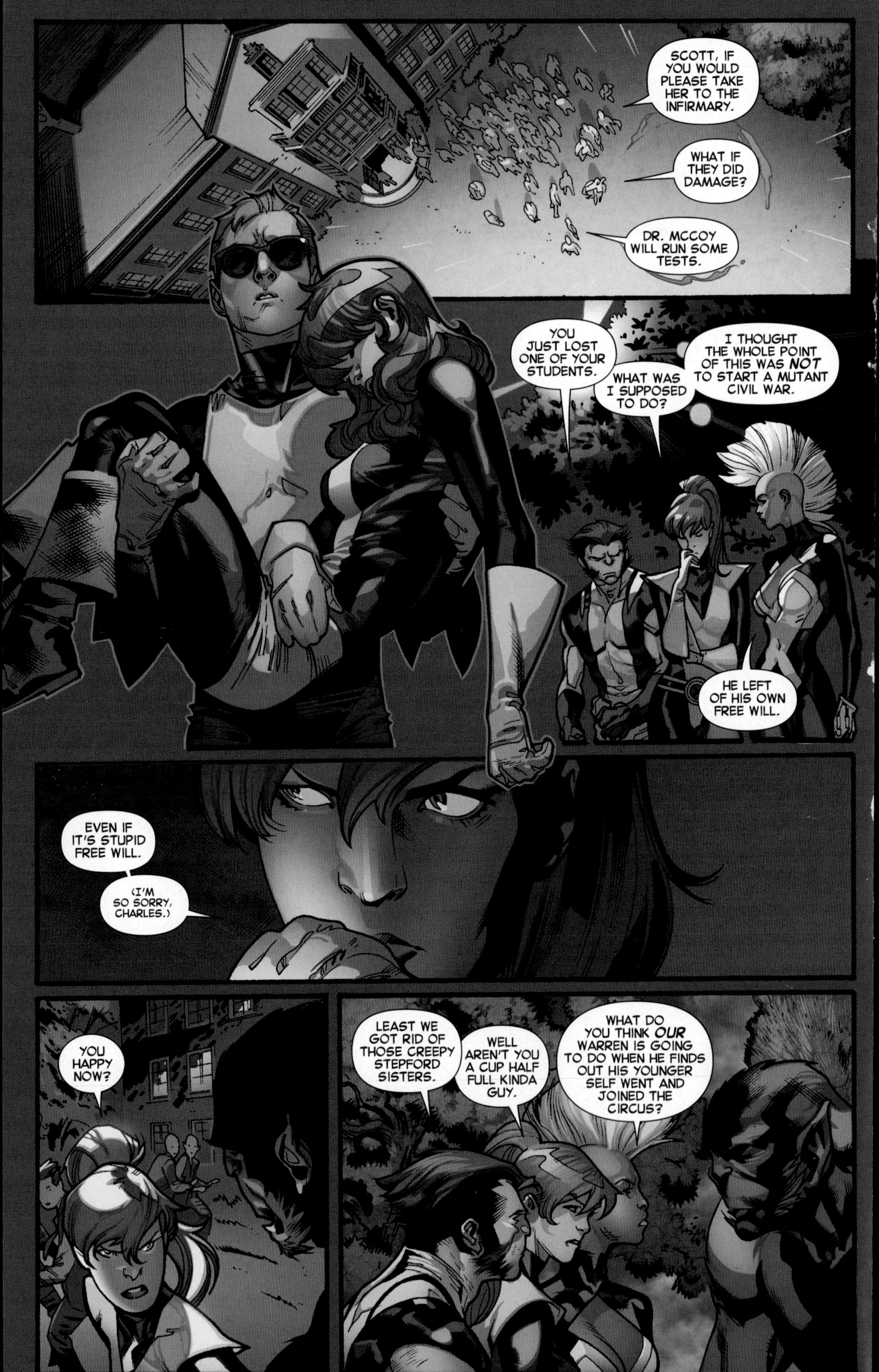
SCOTT, IF YOU WOULD PLEASE TAKE HER TO THE INFIRMARY.
WHAT IF THEY DID DAMAGE?
DR. MCCOY WILL RUN SOME TESTS.
YOU JUST LOST ONE OF YOUR STUDENTS.
WHAT WAS I SUPPOSED TO DO?
I THOUGHT THE WHOLE POINT OF THIS WAS NOT TO START A MUTANT CIVIL WAR.
HE LEFT OF HIS OWN FREE WILL.
EVEN IF IT'S STUPID FREE WILL.
(I'M SO SORRY, CHARLES.)
YOU HAPPY NOW?
LEAST WE GOT RID OF THOSE CREEPY STEPFORD SISTERS.
WELL AREN'T YOU A CUP HALF FULL KINDA GUY.
WHAT DO YOU THINK OUR WARREN IS GOING TO DO WHEN HE FINDS OUT HIS YOUNGER SELF WENT AND JOINED THE CIRCUS?

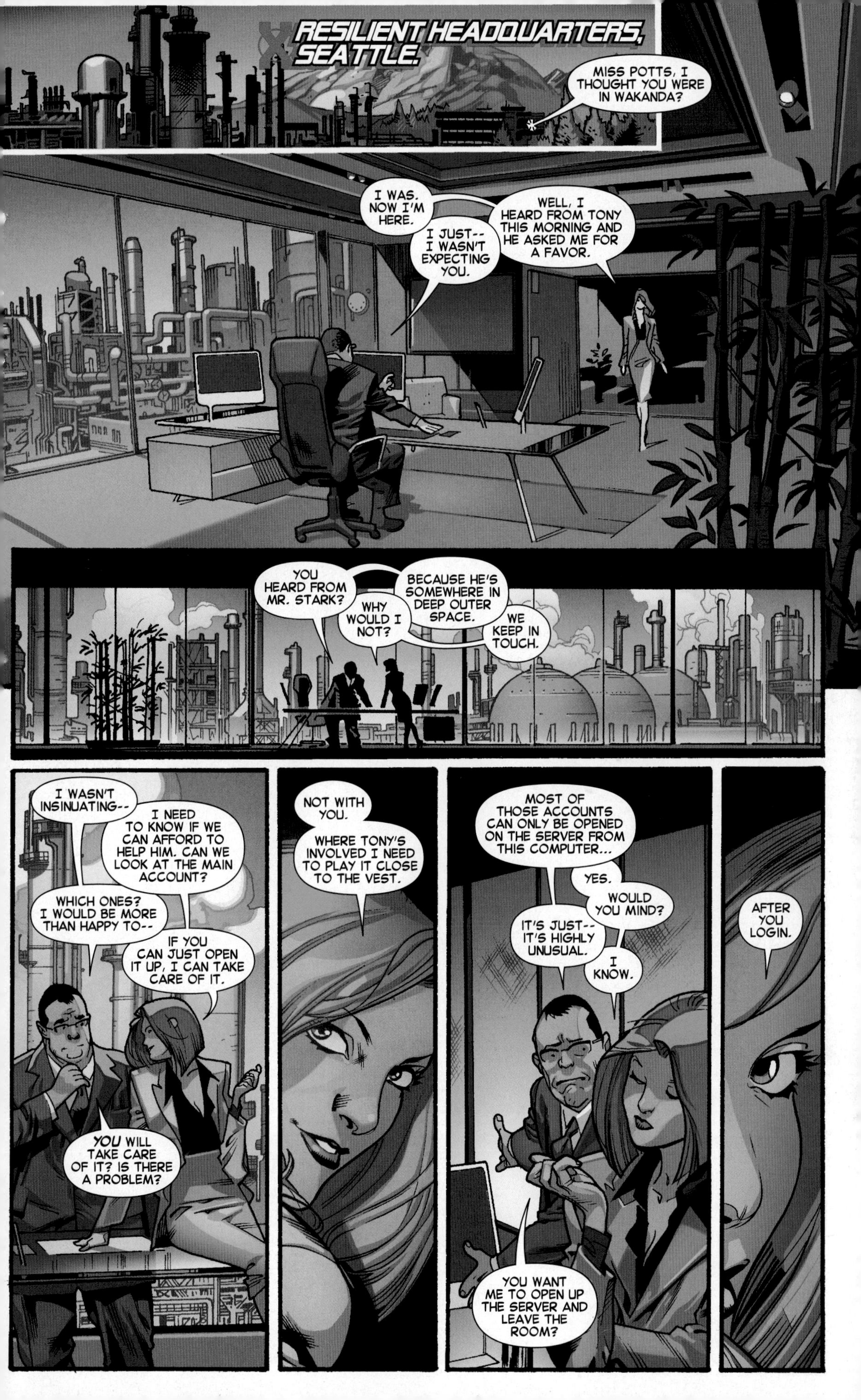
RESILIENT HEADQUARTERS, SEATTLE.
MISS POTTS, I THOUGHT YOU WERE IN WAKANDA?
I WAS. NOW I'M HERE.
I JUST-- I WASN'T EXPECTING YOU.
WELL, I HEARD FROM TONY THIS MORNING AND HE ASKED ME FOR A FAVOR.
YOU HEARD FROM MR. STARK?
WHY WOULD I NOT?
BECAUSE HE'S SOMEWHERE IN DEEP OUTER SPACE.
WE KEEP IN TOUCH.
I WASN'T INSINUATING--
I NEED TO KNOW IF WE CAN AFFORD TO HELP HIM. CAN WE LOOK AT THE MAIN ACCOUNT?
WHICH ONES? I WOULD BE MORE THAN HAPPY TO--
IF YOU CAN JUST OPEN IT UP, I CAN TAKE CARE OF IT.
YOU WILL TAKE CARE OF IT? IS THERE A PROBLEM?
NOT WITH YOU.
WHERE TONY'S INVOLVED I NEED TO PLAY IT CLOSE TO THE VEST.
MOST OF THOSE ACCOUNTS CAN ONLY BE OPENED ON THE SERVER FROM THIS COMPUTER...
YES.
WOULD YOU MIND?
IT'S JUST-- IT'S HIGHLY UNUSUAL.
I KNOW.
YOU WANT ME TO OPEN UP THE SERVER AND LEAVE THE ROOM?
AFTER YOU LOGIN.

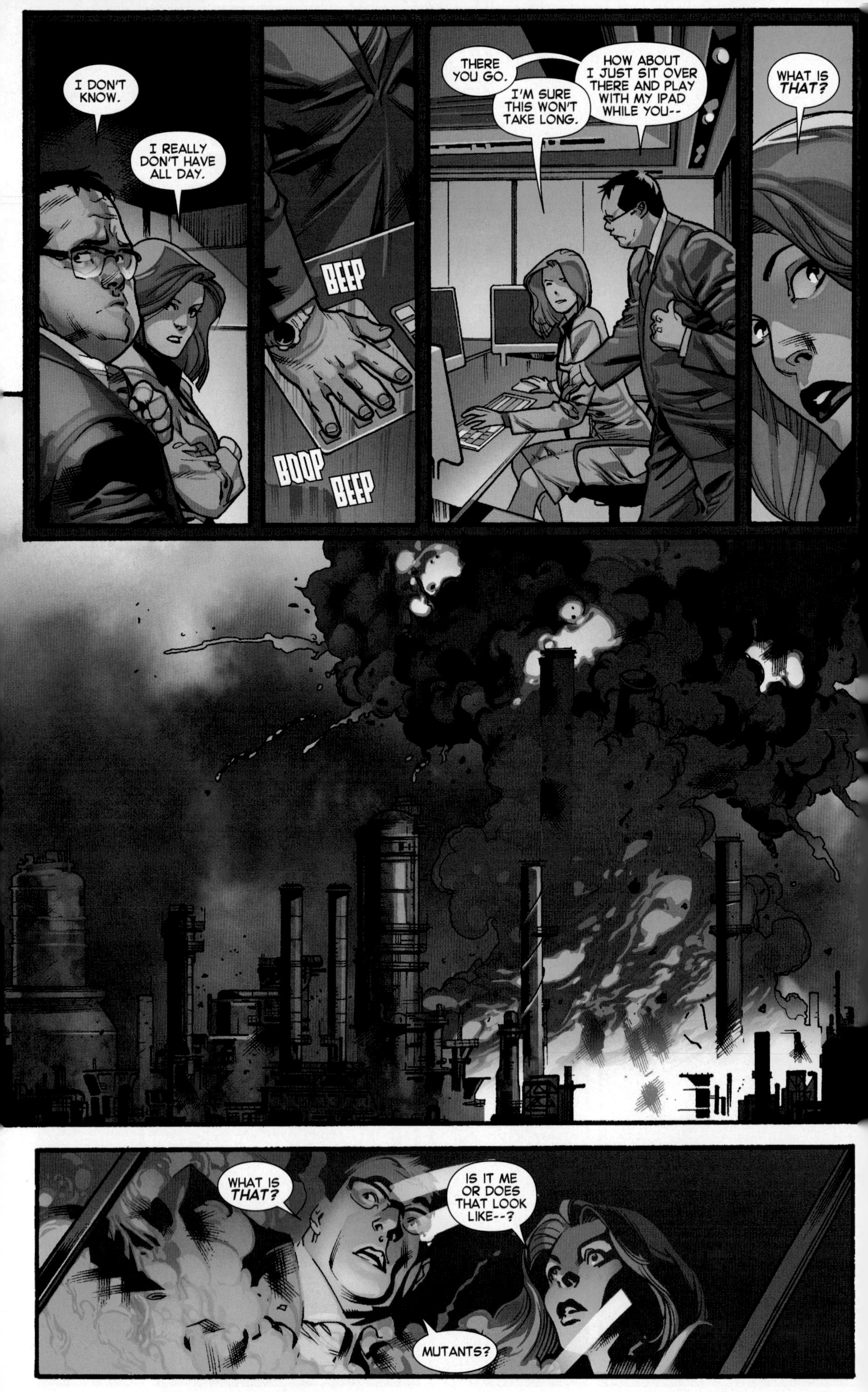

I DON'T KNOW.
I REALLY DON'T HAVE ALL DAY.
BEEP
BOOP
BEEP
THERE YOU GO.
I'M SURE THIS WON'T TAKE LONG.
HOW ABOUT I JUST SIT OVER THERE AND PLAY WITH MY IPAD WHILE YOU--
WHAT IS *THAT?*
WHAT IS *THAT?*
IS IT ME OR DOES THAT LOOK LIKE--?
MUTANTS?

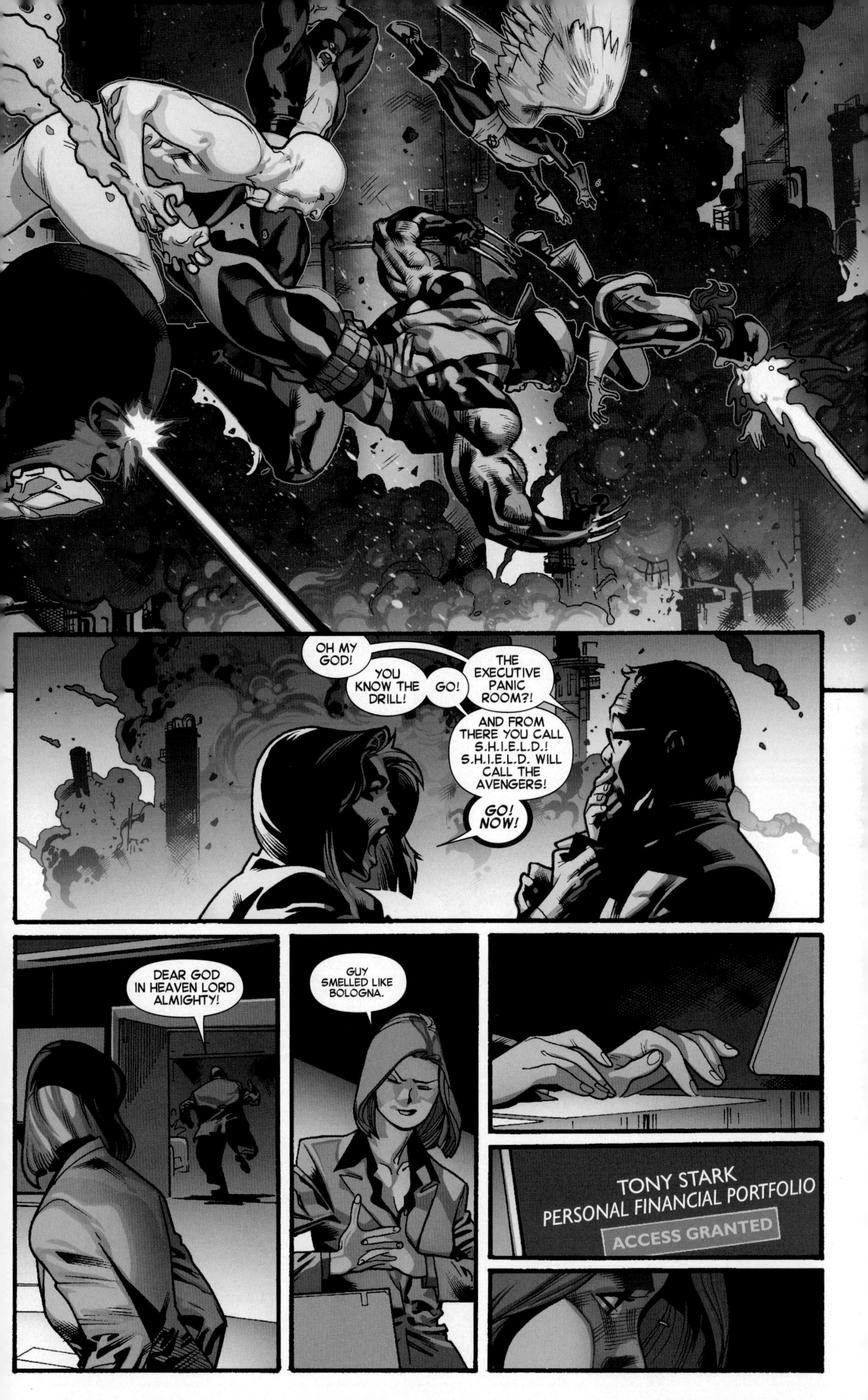

OH MY GOD!
YOU KNOW THE DRILL!
GO!
THE EXECUTIVE PANIC ROOM?!
AND FROM THERE YOU CALL S.H.I.E.L.D.! S.H.I.E.L.D. WILL CALL THE AVENGERS!
GO! NOW!
DEAR GOD IN HEAVEN LORD ALMIGHTY!
GUY SMELLED LIKE BOLOGNA.
TONY STARK
PERSONAL FINANCIAL PORTFOLIO
ACCESS GRANTED

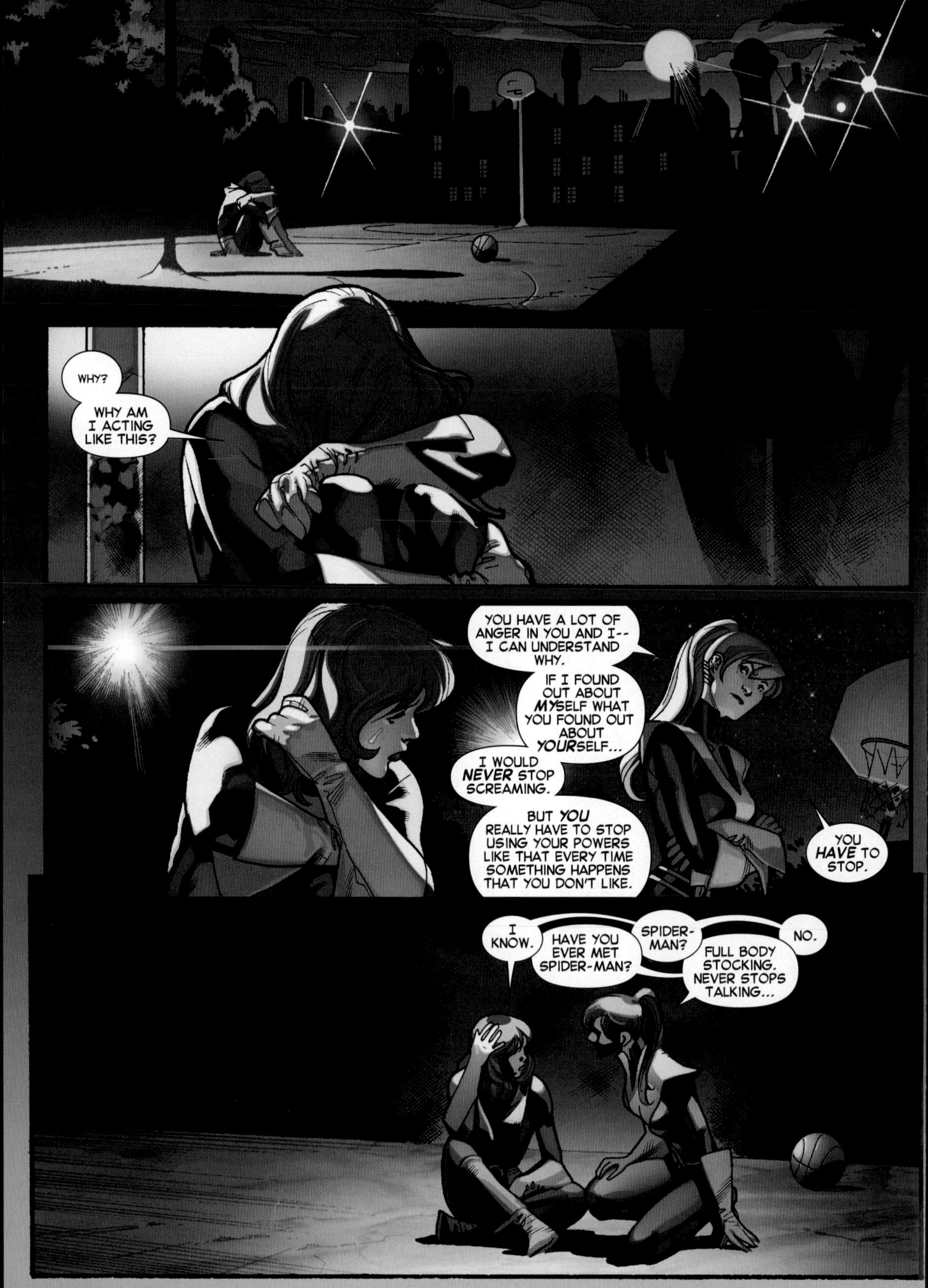
WHY?
WHY AM I ACTING LIKE THIS?
YOU HAVE A LOT OF ANGER IN YOU AND I-- I CAN UNDERSTAND WHY.
IF I FOUND OUT ABOUT MYSELF WHAT YOU FOUND OUT ABOUT YOURSELF...
I WOULD NEVER STOP SCREAMING.
BUT YOU REALLY HAVE TO STOP USING YOUR POWERS LIKE THAT EVERY TIME SOMETHING HAPPENS THAT YOU DON'T LIKE.
YOU HAVE TO STOP.
I KNOW.
HAVE YOU EVER MET SPIDER-MAN?
SPIDER-MAN?
NO.
FULL BODY STOCKING. NEVER STOPS TALKING...

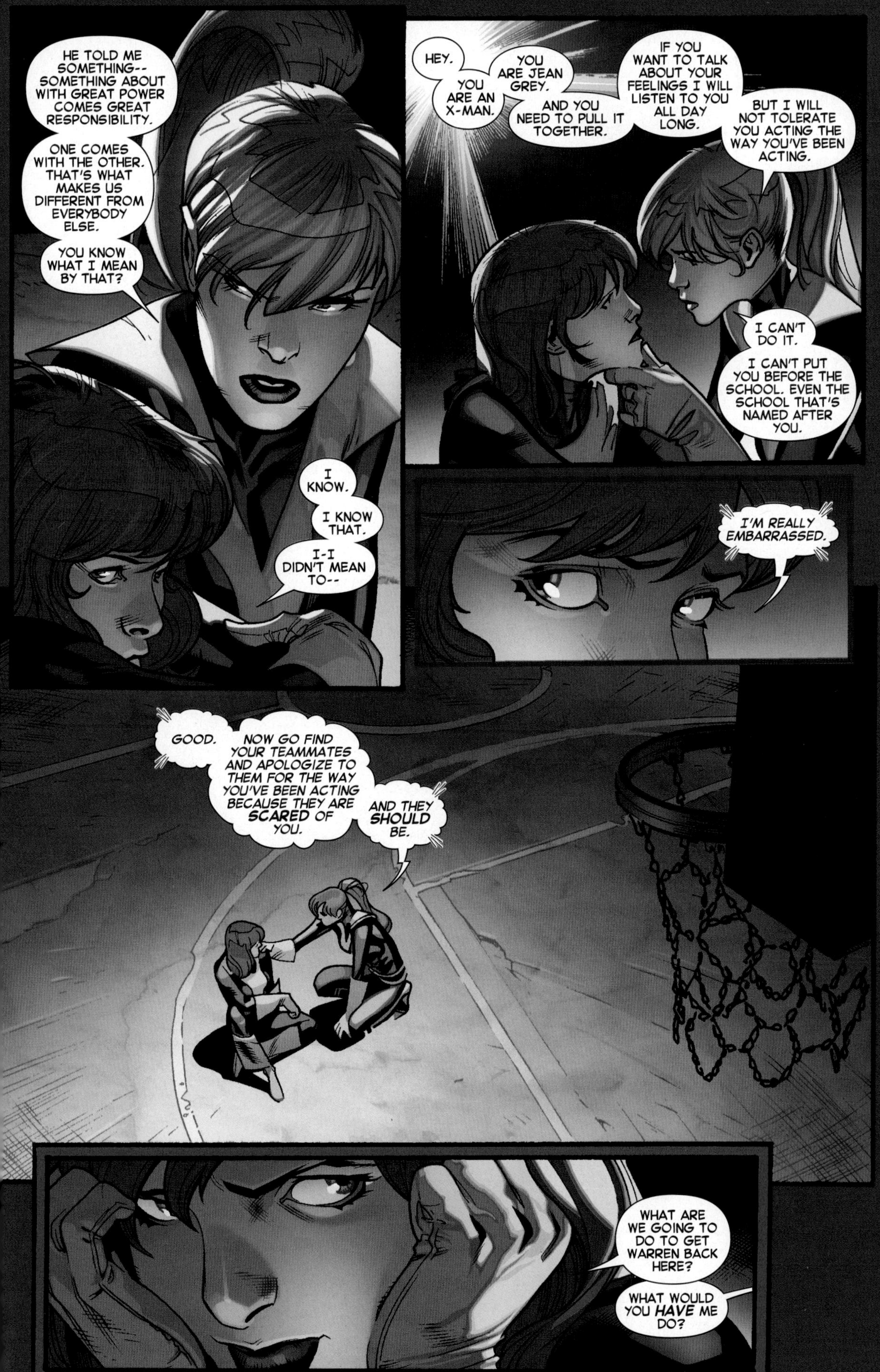
HE TOLD ME SOMETHING-- SOMETHING ABOUT WITH GREAT POWER COMES GREAT RESPONSIBILITY.
ONE COMES WITH THE OTHER. THAT'S WHAT MAKES US DIFFERENT FROM EVERYBODY ELSE.
YOU KNOW WHAT I MEAN BY THAT?
I KNOW.
I KNOW THAT.
I-I DIDN'T MEAN TO--
HEY.
YOU ARE AN X-MAN.
YOU ARE JEAN GREY.
AND YOU NEED TO PULL IT TOGETHER.
IF YOU WANT TO TALK ABOUT YOUR FEELINGS I WILL LISTEN TO YOU ALL DAY LONG.
BUT I WILL NOT TOLERATE YOU ACTING THE WAY YOU'VE BEEN ACTING.
I CAN'T DO IT.
I CAN'T PUT YOU BEFORE THE SCHOOL. EVEN THE SCHOOL THAT'S NAMED AFTER YOU.
I'M REALLY EMBARRASSED.
GOOD.
NOW GO FIND YOUR TEAMMATES AND APOLOGIZE TO THEM FOR THE WAY YOU'VE BEEN ACTING BECAUSE THEY ARE SCARED OF YOU.
AND THEY SHOULD BE.
WHAT ARE WE GOING TO DO TO GET WARREN BACK HERE?
WHAT WOULD YOU HAVE ME DO?

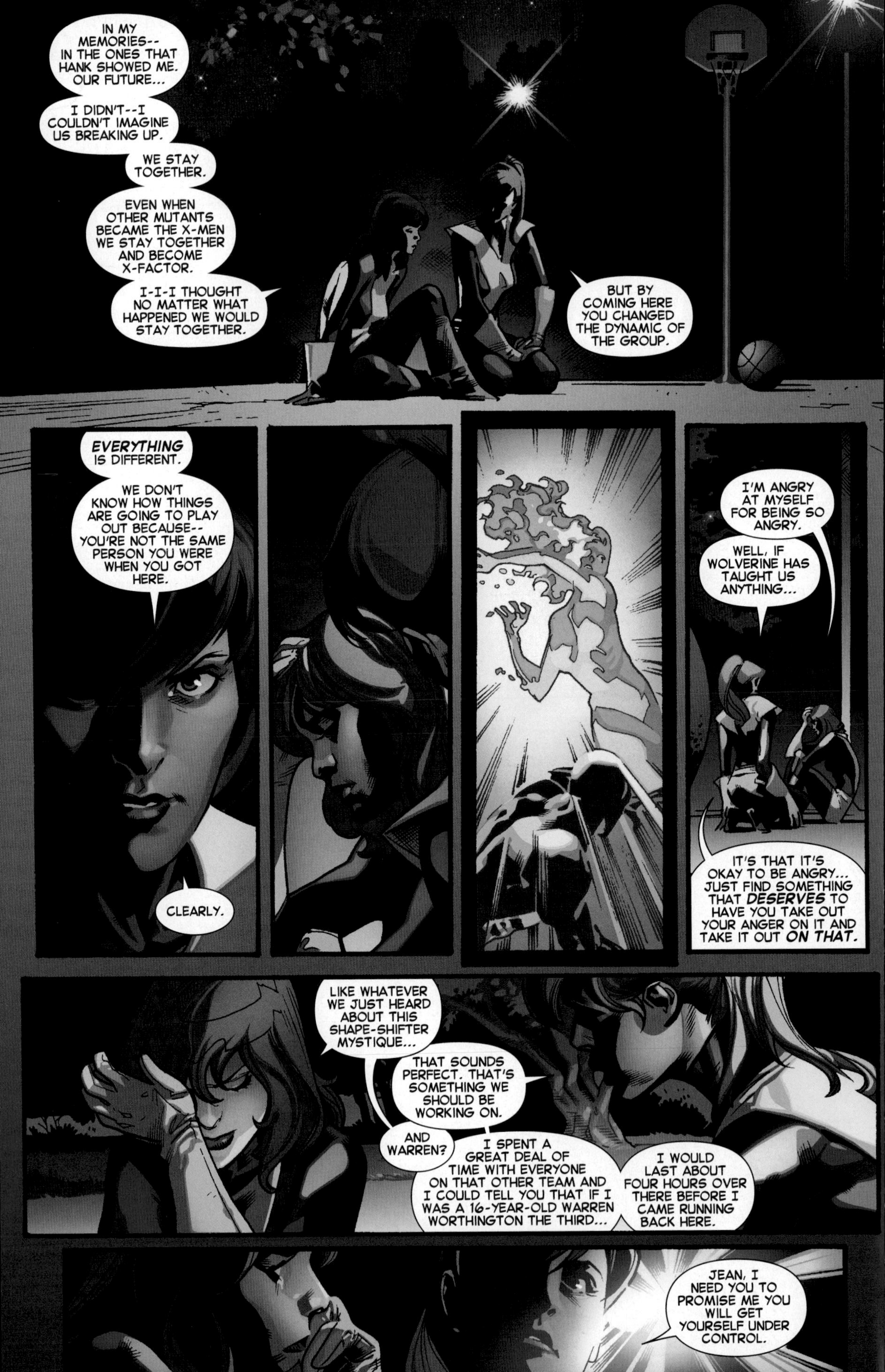
IN MY MEMORIES-- IN THE ONES THAT HANK SHOWED ME. OUR FUTURE...
I DIDN'T--I COULDN'T IMAGINE US BREAKING UP.
WE STAY TOGETHER.
EVEN WHEN OTHER MUTANTS BECAME THE X-MEN WE STAY TOGETHER AND BECOME X-FACTOR.
I-I-I THOUGHT NO MATTER WHAT HAPPENED WE WOULD STAY TOGETHER.
BUT BY COMING HERE YOU CHANGED THE DYNAMIC OF THE GROUP.
EVERYTHING IS DIFFERENT.
WE DON'T KNOW HOW THINGS ARE GOING TO PLAY OUT BECAUSE-- YOU'RE NOT THE SAME PERSON YOU WERE WHEN YOU GOT HERE.
CLEARLY.
I'M ANGRY AT MYSELF FOR BEING SO ANGRY.
WELL, IF WOLVERINE HAS TAUGHT US ANYTHING...
IT'S THAT IT'S OKAY TO BE ANGRY... JUST FIND SOMETHING THAT *DESERVES* TO HAVE YOU TAKE OUT YOUR ANGER ON IT AND TAKE IT OUT *ON THAT.*
LIKE WHATEVER WE JUST HEARD ABOUT THIS SHAPE-SHIFTER MYSTIQUE...
THAT SOUNDS PERFECT. THAT'S SOMETHING WE SHOULD BE WORKING ON.
AND WARREN?
I SPENT A GREAT DEAL OF TIME WITH EVERYONE ON THAT OTHER TEAM AND I COULD TELL YOU THAT IF I WAS A 16-YEAR-OLD WARREN WORTHINGTON THE THIRD...
I WOULD LAST ABOUT FOUR HOURS OVER THERE BEFORE I CAME RUNNING BACK HERE.
JEAN, I NEED YOU TO PROMISE ME YOU WILL GET YOURSELF UNDER CONTROL.

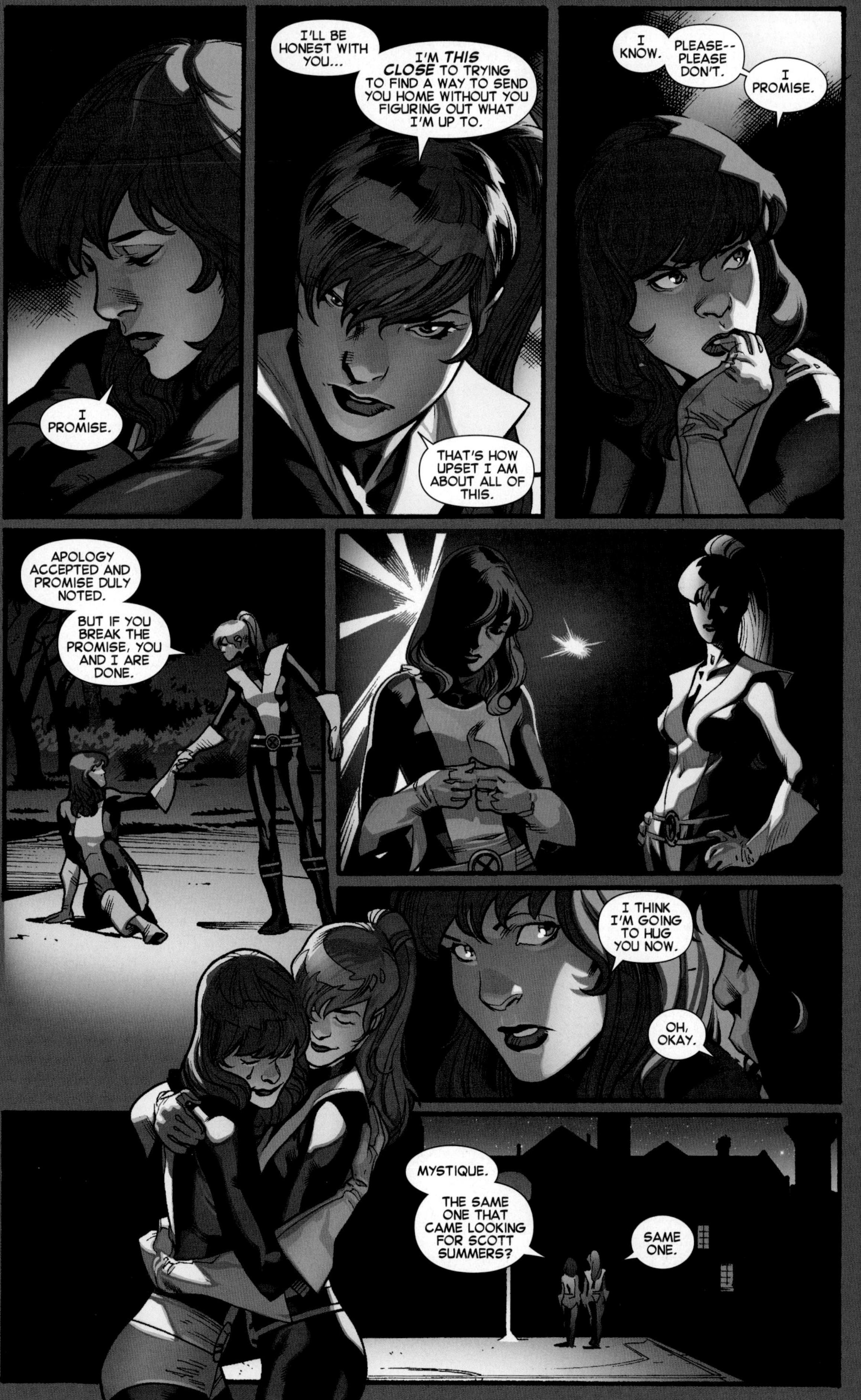
I PROMISE.
I'LL BE HONEST WITH YOU...
I'M THIS CLOSE TO TRYING TO FIND A WAY TO SEND YOU HOME WITHOUT YOU FIGURING OUT WHAT I'M UP TO.
THAT'S HOW UPSET I AM ABOUT ALL OF THIS.
I KNOW.
PLEASE-- PLEASE DON'T.
I PROMISE.
APOLOGY ACCEPTED AND PROMISE DULY NOTED.
BUT IF YOU BREAK THE PROMISE, YOU AND I ARE DONE.
I THINK I'M GOING TO HUG YOU NOW.
OH, OKAY.
MYSTIQUE.
THE SAME ONE THAT CAME LOOKING FOR SCOTT SUMMERS?
SAME ONE.

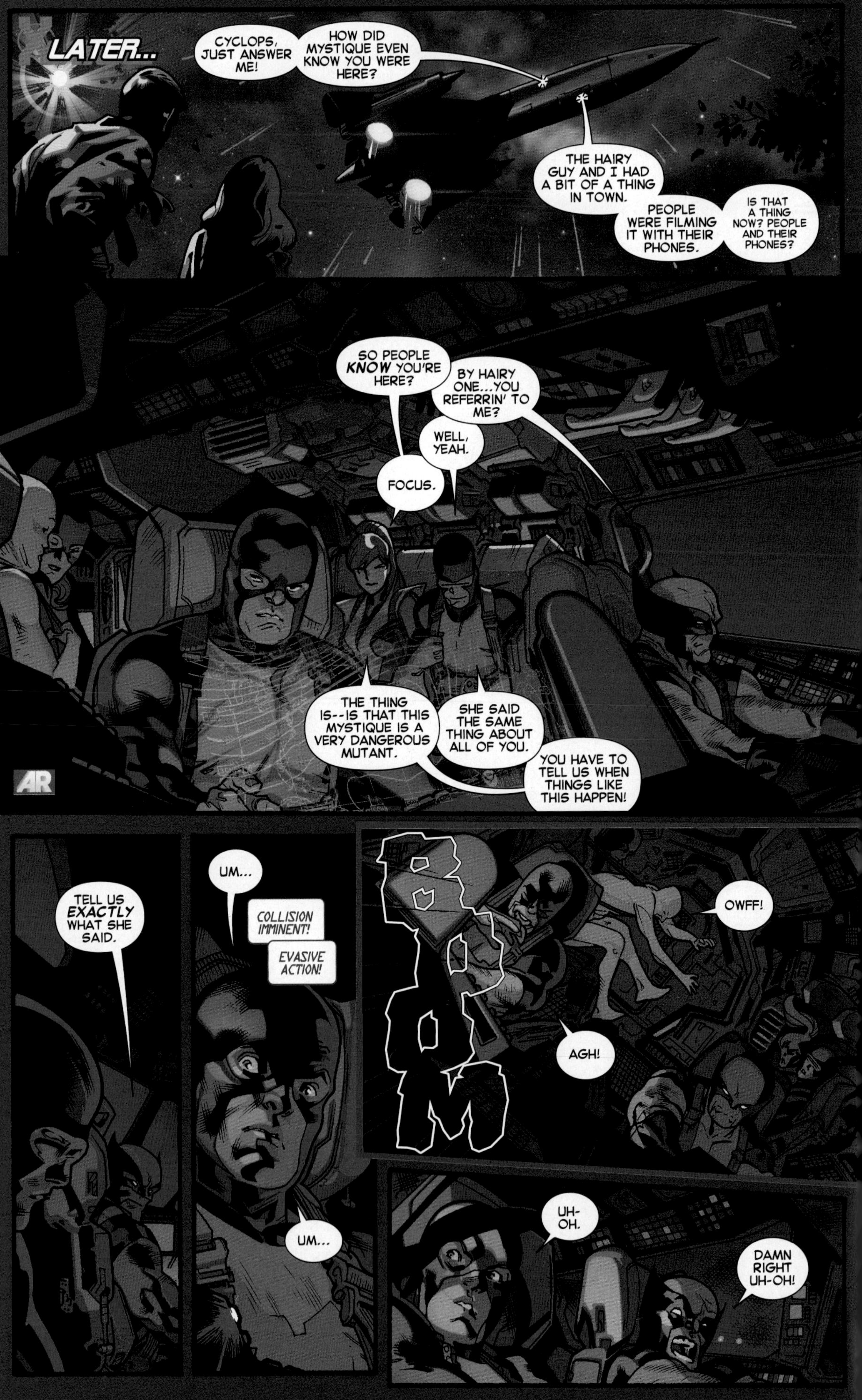
LATER...
CYCLOPS, JUST ANSWER ME!
HOW DID MYSTIQUE EVEN KNOW YOU WERE HERE?
THE HAIRY GUY AND I HAD A BIT OF A THING IN TOWN.
PEOPLE WERE FILMING IT WITH THEIR PHONES.
IS THAT A THING NOW? PEOPLE AND THEIR PHONES?
SO PEOPLE KNOW YOU'RE HERE?
BY HAIRY ONE...YOU REFERRIN' TO ME?
WELL, YEAH.
FOCUS.
THE THING IS--IS THAT THIS MYSTIQUE IS A VERY DANGEROUS MUTANT.
SHE SAID THE SAME THING ABOUT ALL OF YOU.
YOU HAVE TO TELL US WHEN THINGS LIKE THIS HAPPEN!
TELL US EXACTLY WHAT SHE SAID.
UM...
COLLISION IMMINENT!
EVASIVE ACTION!
UM...
BOOM
OWFF!
AGH!
UH-OH.
DAMN RIGHT UH-OH!

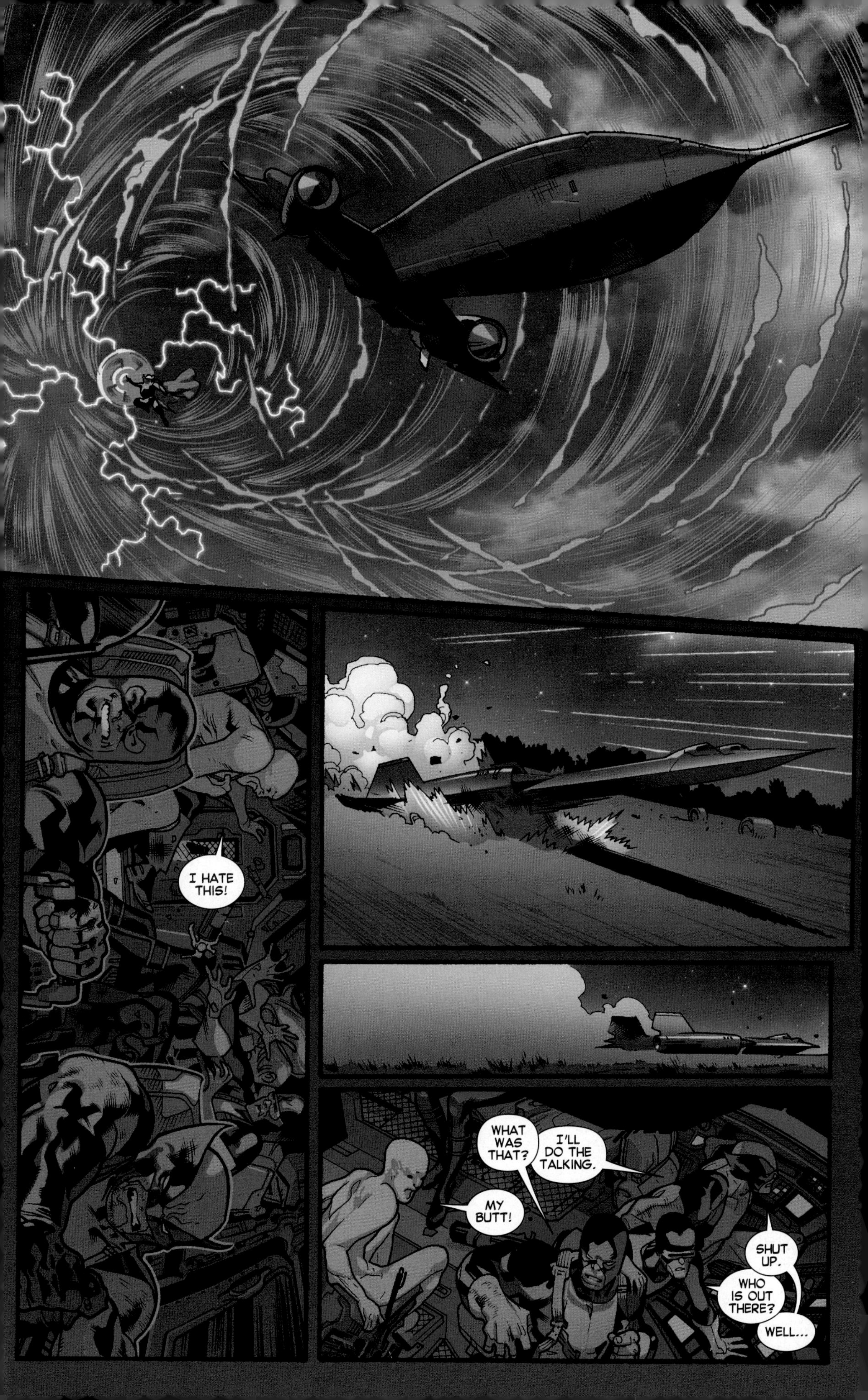
I HATE THIS!
WHAT WAS THAT?
I'LL DO THE TALKING.
MY BUTT!
SHUT UP.
WHO IS OUT THERE?
WELL...

"YOUR BROTHER AND HIS...
UNCANNY AVENGERS
COME OUT WITH YOUR HANDS UP!
YOU ARE IN A LOT OF TROUBLE!
DON'T MAKE IT ANY WORSE FOR YOURSELVES!
AR

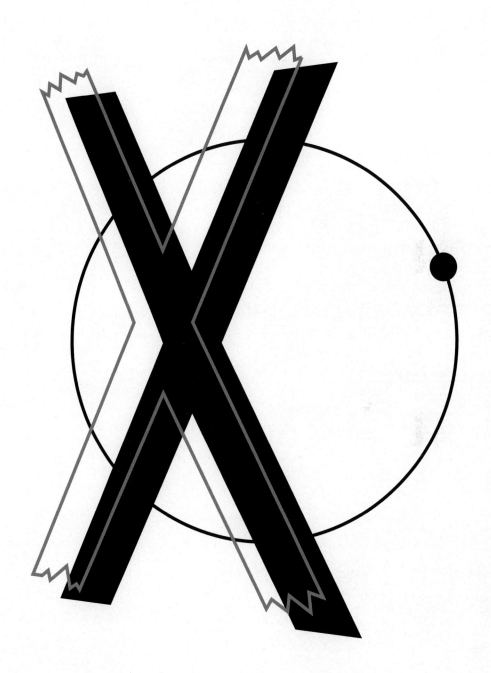

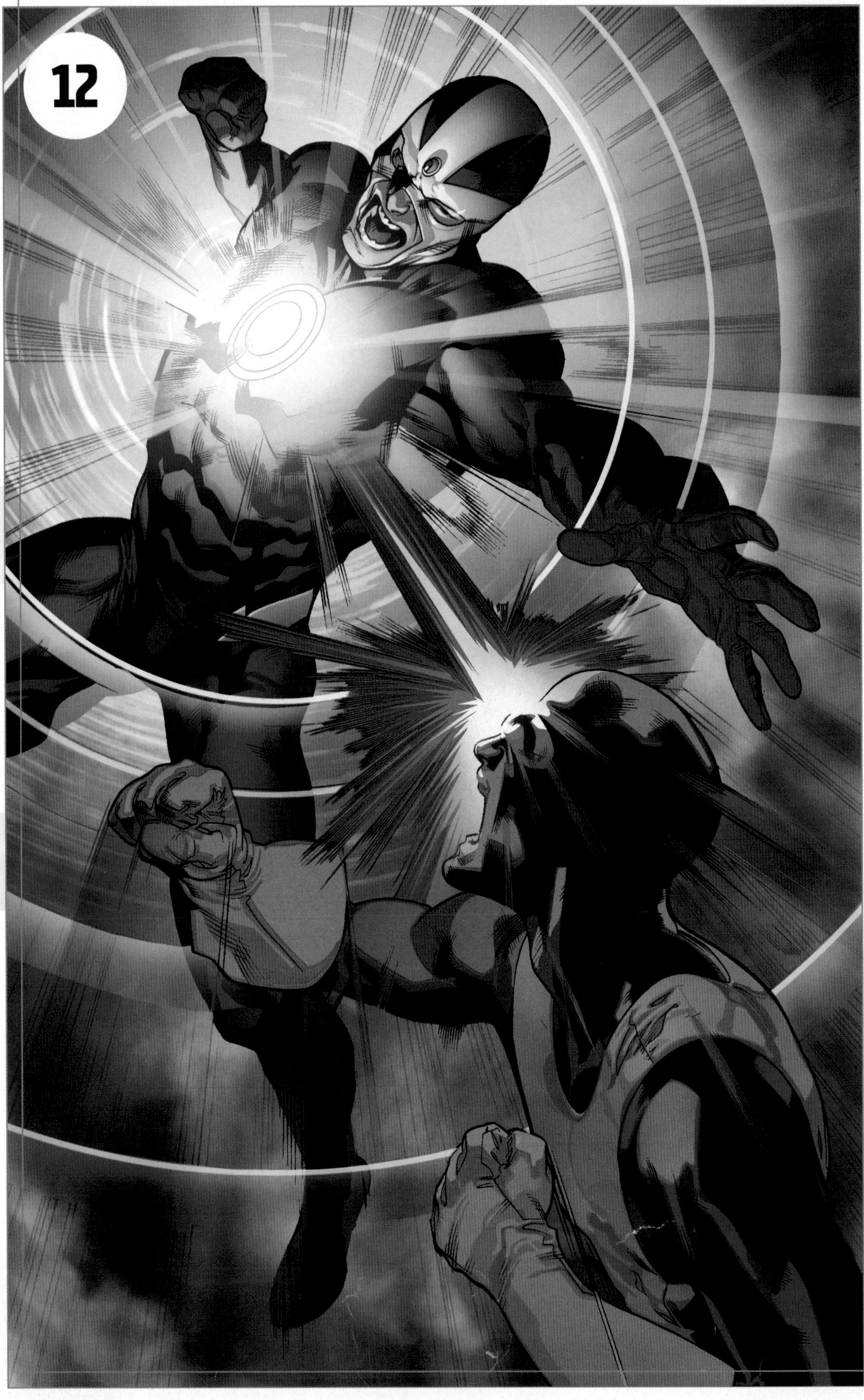
12

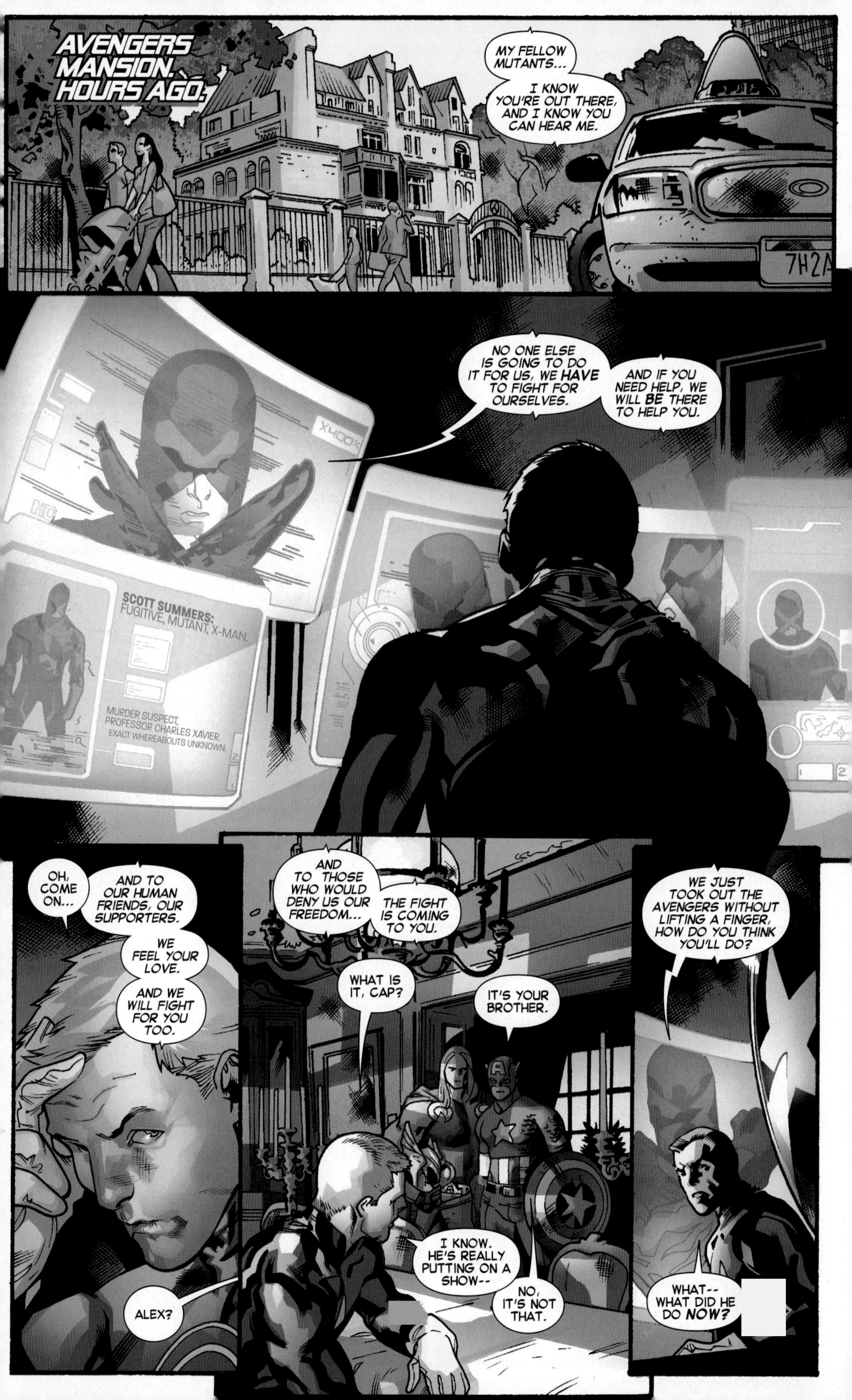
AVENGERS MANSION. HOURS AGO:
MY FELLOW MUTANTS...
I KNOW YOU'RE OUT THERE, AND I KNOW YOU CAN HEAR ME.
NO ONE ELSE IS GOING TO DO IT FOR US, WE HAVE TO FIGHT FOR OURSELVES.
AND IF YOU NEED HELP, WE WILL BE THERE TO HELP YOU.
X400%
SCOTT SUMMERS:
FUGITIVE, MUTANT, X-MAN.
MURDER SUSPECT, PROFESSOR CHARLES XAVIER. EXACT WHEREABOUTS UNKNOWN.
OH, COME ON...
AND TO OUR HUMAN FRIENDS, OUR SUPPORTERS.
WE FEEL YOUR LOVE.
AND WE WILL FIGHT FOR YOU TOO.
ALEX?
AND TO THOSE WHO WOULD DENY US OUR FREEDOM...
THE FIGHT IS COMING TO YOU.
WHAT IS IT, CAP?
IT'S YOUR BROTHER.
I KNOW. HE'S REALLY PUTTING ON A SHOW--
NO, IT'S NOT THAT.
WE JUST TOOK OUT THE AVENGERS WITHOUT LIFTING A FINGER, HOW DO YOU THINK YOU'LL DO?
WHAT-- WHAT DID HE DO NOW?

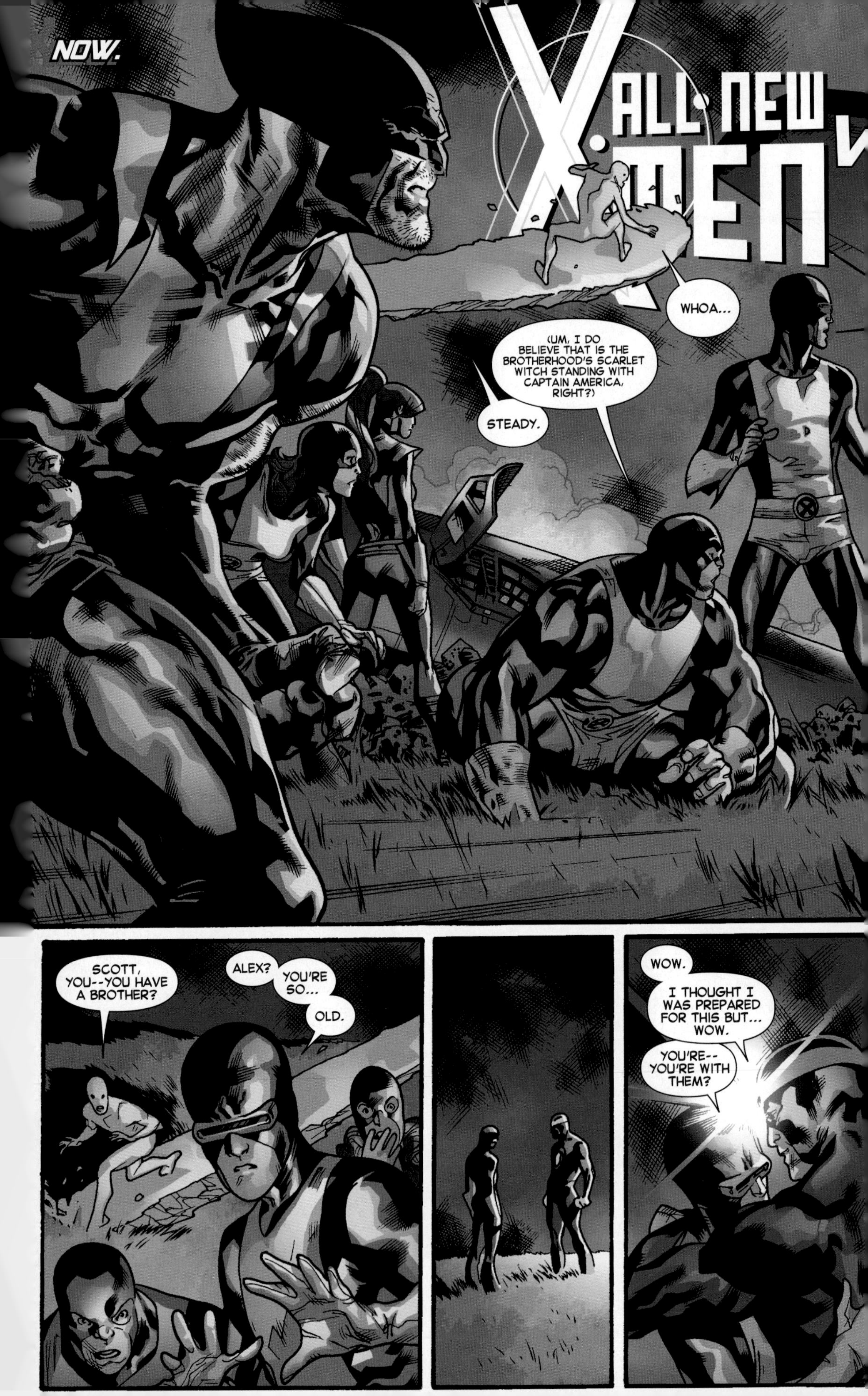

NOW.
ALL NEW X-MEN
WHOA...
(UM, I DO BELIEVE THAT IS THE BROTHERHOOD'S SCARLET WITCH STANDING WITH CAPTAIN AMERICA, RIGHT?)
STEADY.
SCOTT, YOU--YOU HAVE A BROTHER?
ALEX? YOU'RE SO...
OLD.
WOW.
I THOUGHT I WAS PREPARED FOR THIS BUT... WOW.
YOU'RE--YOU'RE WITH THEM?

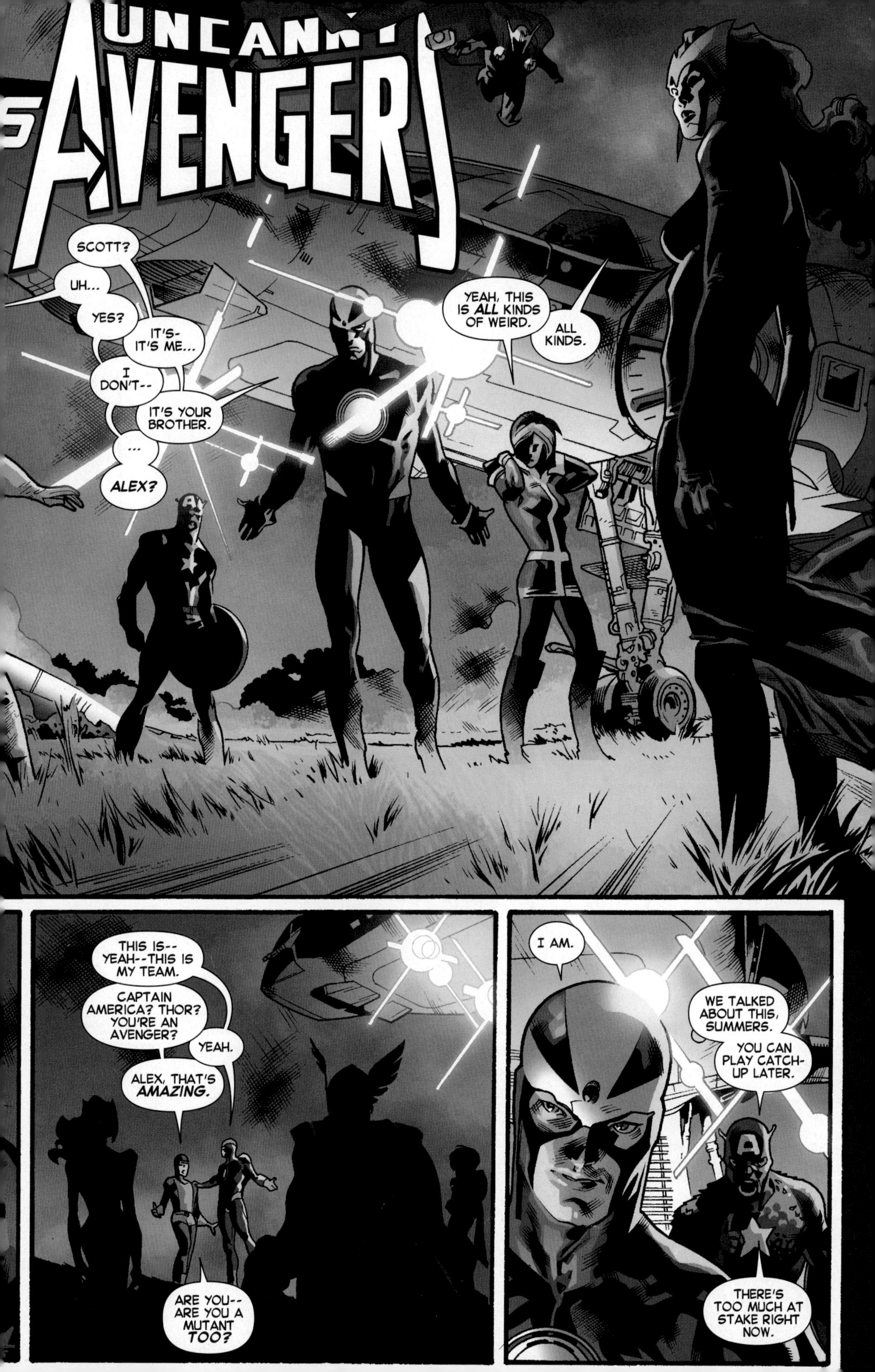
UNCANNY AVENGERS
SCOTT?
UH...
YES?
IT'S- IT'S ME...
I DON'T--
IT'S YOUR BROTHER.
...
ALEX?
YEAH, THIS IS ALL KINDS OF WEIRD.
ALL KINDS.
THIS IS-- YEAH--THIS IS MY TEAM.
CAPTAIN AMERICA? THOR? YOU'RE AN AVENGER?
YEAH.
ALEX, THAT'S AMAZING.
ARE YOU-- ARE YOU A MUTANT TOO?
I AM.
WE TALKED ABOUT THIS, SUMMERS.
YOU CAN PLAY CATCH-UP LATER.
THERE'S TOO MUCH AT STAKE RIGHT NOW.

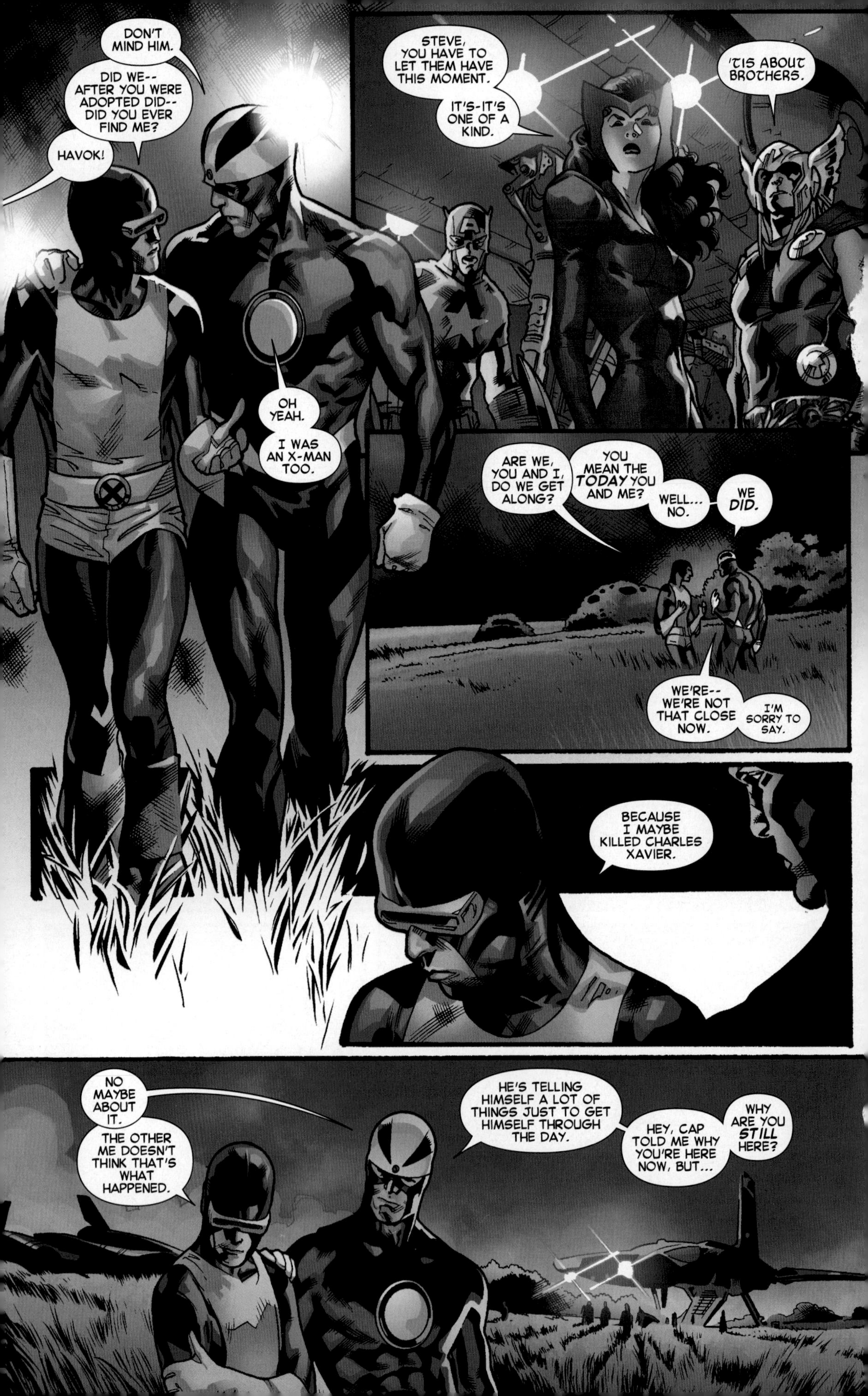
DON'T MIND HIM.
DID WE-- AFTER YOU WERE ADOPTED DID-- DID YOU EVER FIND ME?
HAVOK!
STEVE, YOU HAVE TO LET THEM HAVE THIS MOMENT.
IT'S-IT'S ONE OF A KIND.
'TIS ABOUT BROTHERS.
OH YEAH.
I WAS AN X-MAN TOO.
ARE WE, YOU AND I, DO WE GET ALONG?
YOU MEAN THE TODAY YOU AND ME?
WELL... NO.
WE DID.
WE'RE-- WE'RE NOT THAT CLOSE NOW.
I'M SORRY TO SAY.
BECAUSE I MAYBE KILLED CHARLES XAVIER.
NO MAYBE ABOUT IT.
THE OTHER ME DOESN'T THINK THAT'S WHAT HAPPENED.
HE'S TELLING HIMSELF A LOT OF THINGS JUST TO GET HIMSELF THROUGH THE DAY.
HEY, CAP TOLD ME WHY YOU'RE HERE NOW, BUT...
WHY ARE YOU STILL HERE?

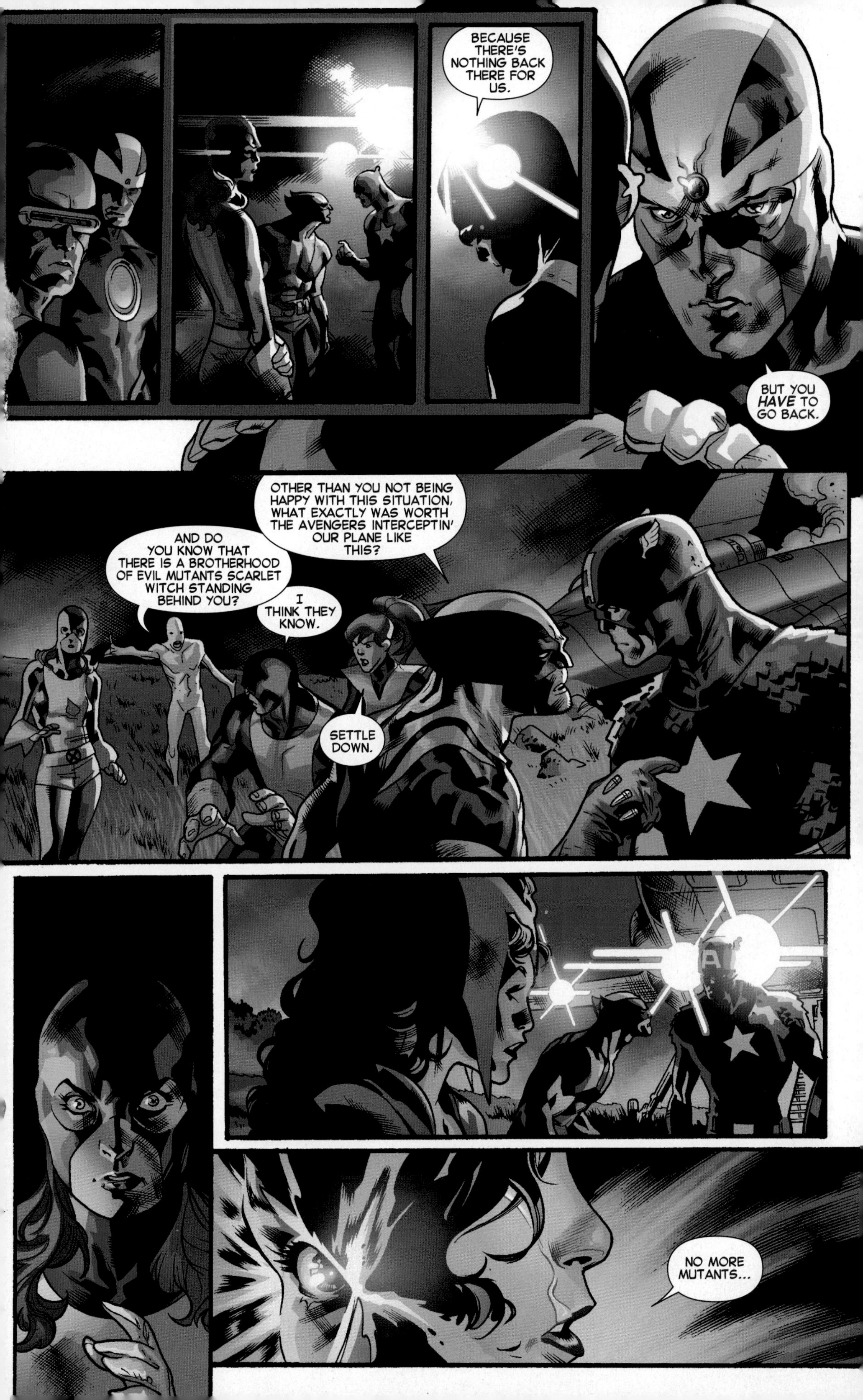
BECAUSE THERE'S NOTHING BACK THERE FOR US.
BUT YOU HAVE TO GO BACK.
AND DO YOU KNOW THAT THERE IS A BROTHERHOOD OF EVIL MUTANTS SCARLET WITCH STANDING BEHIND YOU?
OTHER THAN YOU NOT BEING HAPPY WITH THIS SITUATION, WHAT EXACTLY WAS WORTH THE AVENGERS INTERCEPTIN' OUR PLANE LIKE THIS?
I THINK THEY KNOW.
SETTLE DOWN.
NO MORE MUTANTS...

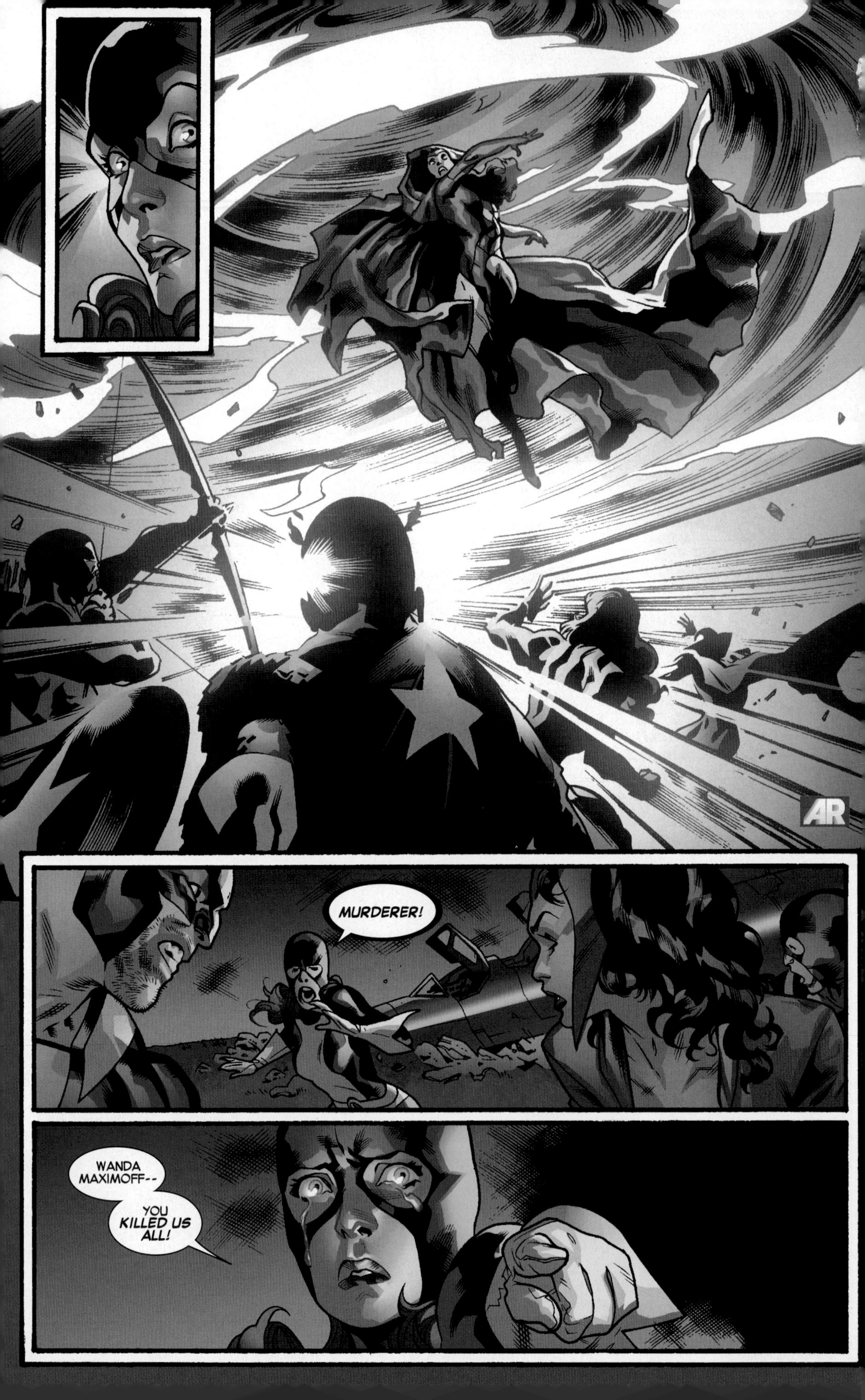
AR
MURDERER!
WANDA MAXIMOFF--
YOU KILLED US ALL!

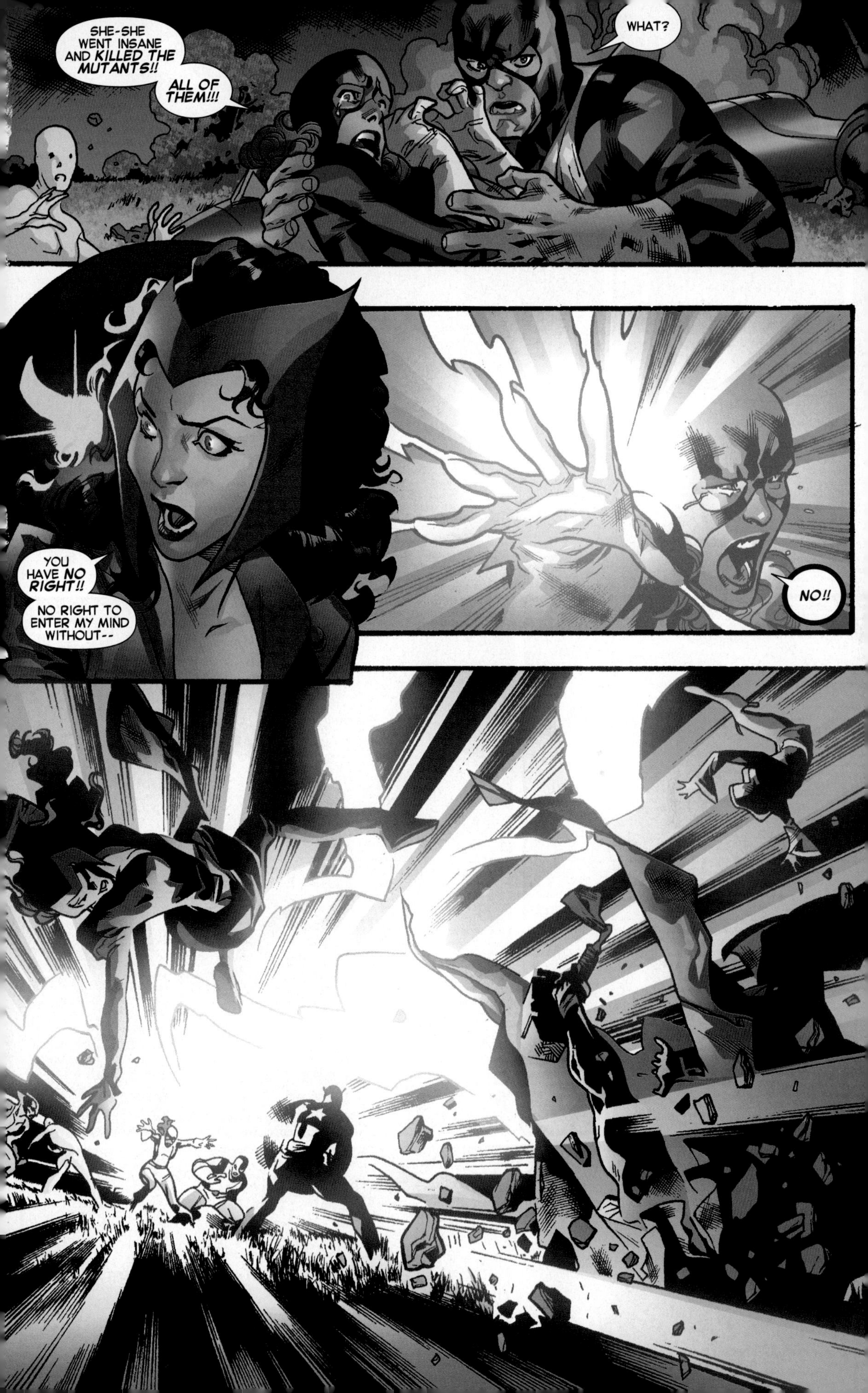
SHE-SHE WENT INSANE AND KILLED THE MUTANTS!!
ALL OF THEM!!!
WHAT?
YOU HAVE NO RIGHT!!
NO RIGHT TO ENTER MY MIND WITHOUT--
NO!!

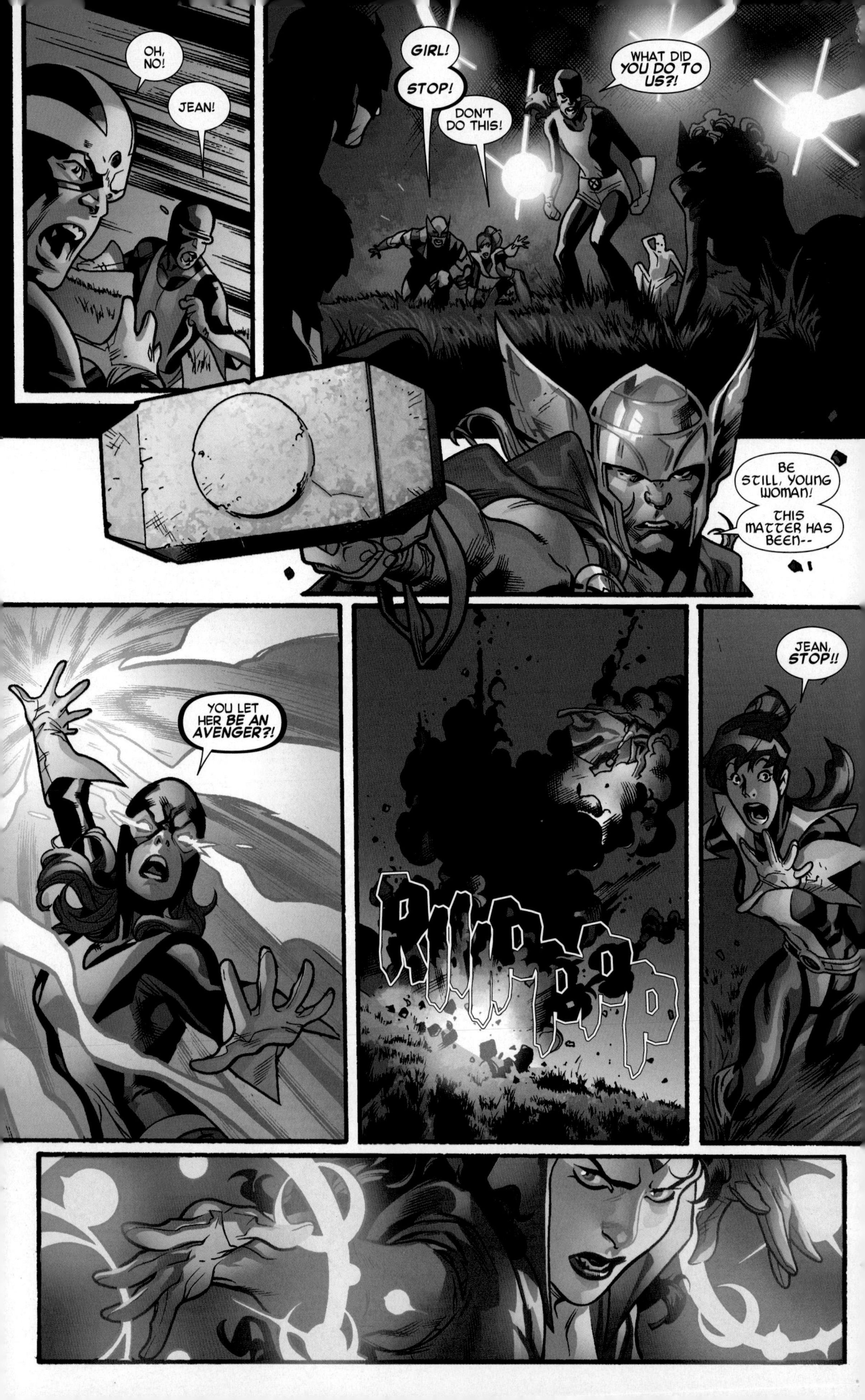
OH, NO!
JEAN!
GIRL!
STOP!
DON'T DO THIS!
WHAT DID YOU DO TO US?!
BE STILL, YOUNG WOMAN!
THIS MATTER HAS BEEN--
YOU LET HER BE AN AVENGER?!
JEAN, STOP!!

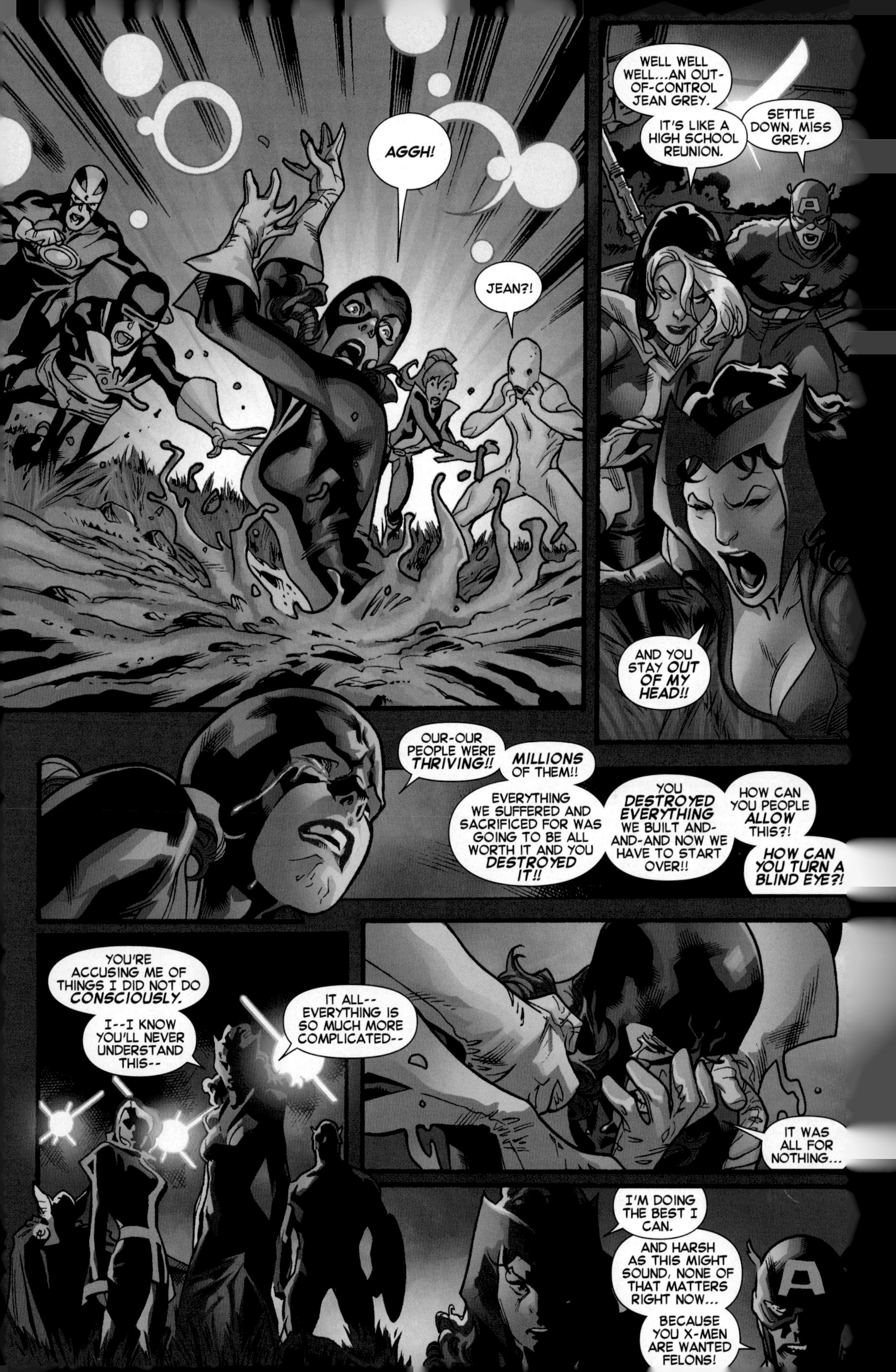
AGGH!
JEAN?!
WELL WELL WELL...AN OUT-OF-CONTROL JEAN GREY.
IT'S LIKE A HIGH SCHOOL REUNION.
SETTLE DOWN, MISS GREY.
AND YOU STAY OUT OF MY HEAD!!
OUR-OUR PEOPLE WERE THRIVING!!
MILLIONS OF THEM!!
EVERYTHING WE SUFFERED AND SACRIFICED FOR WAS GOING TO BE ALL WORTH IT AND YOU DESTROYED IT!!
YOU DESTROYED EVERYTHING WE BUILT AND-AND-AND NOW WE HAVE TO START OVER!!
HOW CAN YOU PEOPLE ALLOW THIS?!
HOW CAN YOU TURN A BLIND EYE?!
YOU'RE ACCUSING ME OF THINGS I DID NOT DO CONSCIOUSLY.
I--I KNOW YOU'LL NEVER UNDERSTAND THIS--
IT ALL--EVERYTHING IS SO MUCH MORE COMPLICATED--
IT WAS ALL FOR NOTHING...
I'M DOING THE BEST I CAN.
AND HARSH AS THIS MIGHT SOUND, NONE OF THAT MATTERS RIGHT NOW...
BECAUSE YOU X-MEN ARE WANTED FELONS!

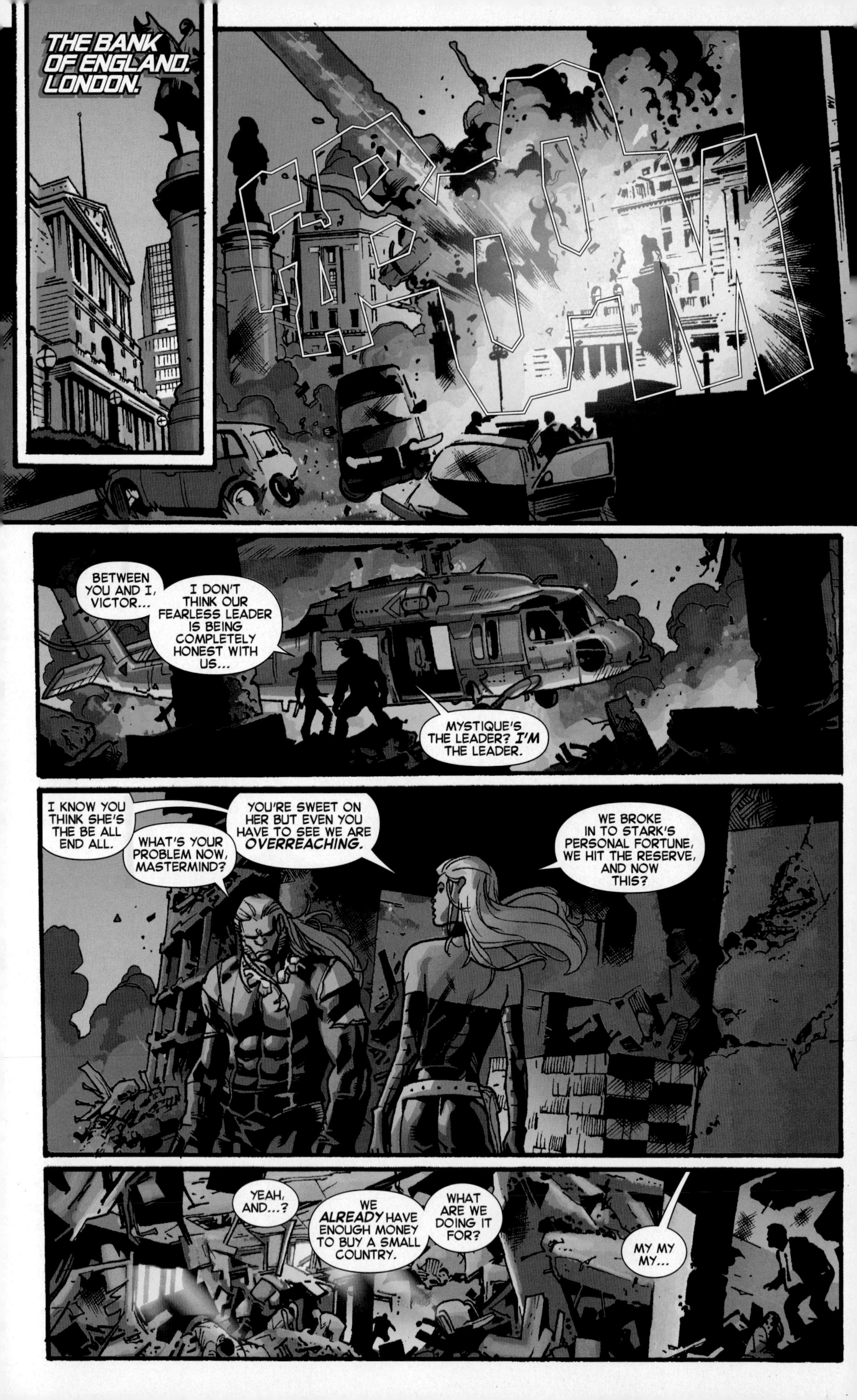
THE BANK OF ENGLAND. LONDON.
BETWEEN YOU AND I, VICTOR...
I DON'T THINK OUR FEARLESS LEADER IS BEING COMPLETELY HONEST WITH US...
MYSTIQUE'S THE LEADER? *I'M* THE LEADER.
WHAT'S YOUR PROBLEM NOW, MASTERMIND?
I KNOW YOU THINK SHE'S THE BE ALL END ALL.
YOU'RE SWEET ON HER BUT EVEN YOU HAVE TO SEE WE ARE *OVERREACHING.*
WE BROKE IN TO STARK'S PERSONAL FORTUNE, WE HIT THE RESERVE, AND NOW THIS?
YEAH, AND...?
WE *ALREADY* HAVE ENOUGH MONEY TO BUY A SMALL COUNTRY.
WHAT ARE WE DOING IT FOR?
MY MY MY...

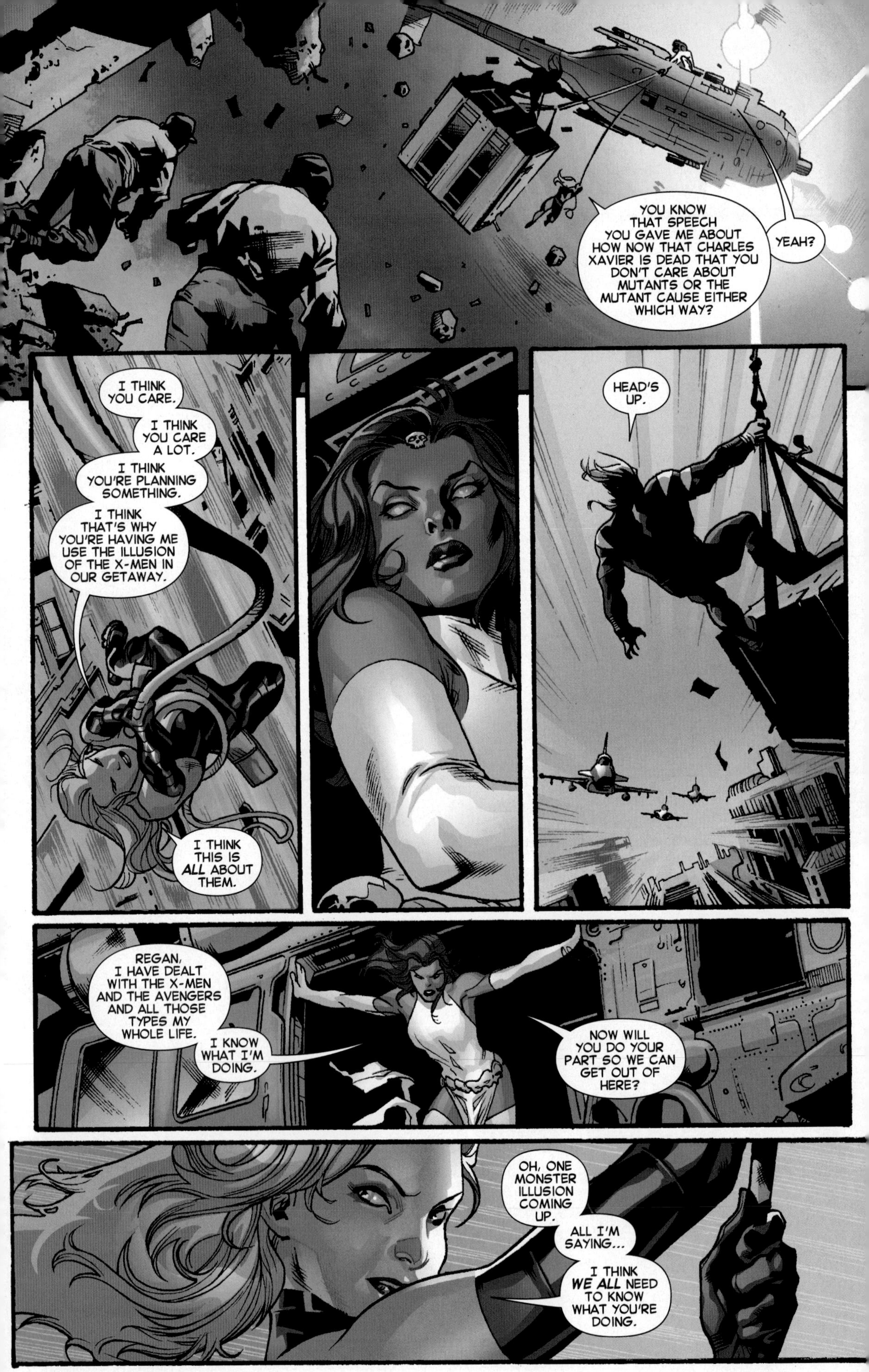

YOU KNOW THAT SPEECH YOU GAVE ME ABOUT HOW NOW THAT CHARLES XAVIER IS DEAD THAT YOU DON'T CARE ABOUT MUTANTS OR THE MUTANT CAUSE EITHER WHICH WAY?
YEAH?
I THINK YOU CARE.
I THINK YOU CARE A LOT.
I THINK YOU'RE PLANNING SOMETHING.
I THINK THAT'S WHY YOU'RE HAVING ME USE THE ILLUSION OF THE X-MEN IN OUR GETAWAY.
I THINK THIS IS ALL ABOUT THEM.
HEAD'S UP.
REGAN, I HAVE DEALT WITH THE X-MEN AND THE AVENGERS AND ALL THOSE TYPES MY WHOLE LIFE.
I KNOW WHAT I'M DOING.
NOW WILL YOU DO YOUR PART SO WE CAN GET OUT OF HERE?
OH, ONE MONSTER ILLUSION COMING UP.
ALL I'M SAYING...
I THINK WE ALL NEED TO KNOW WHAT YOU'RE DOING.

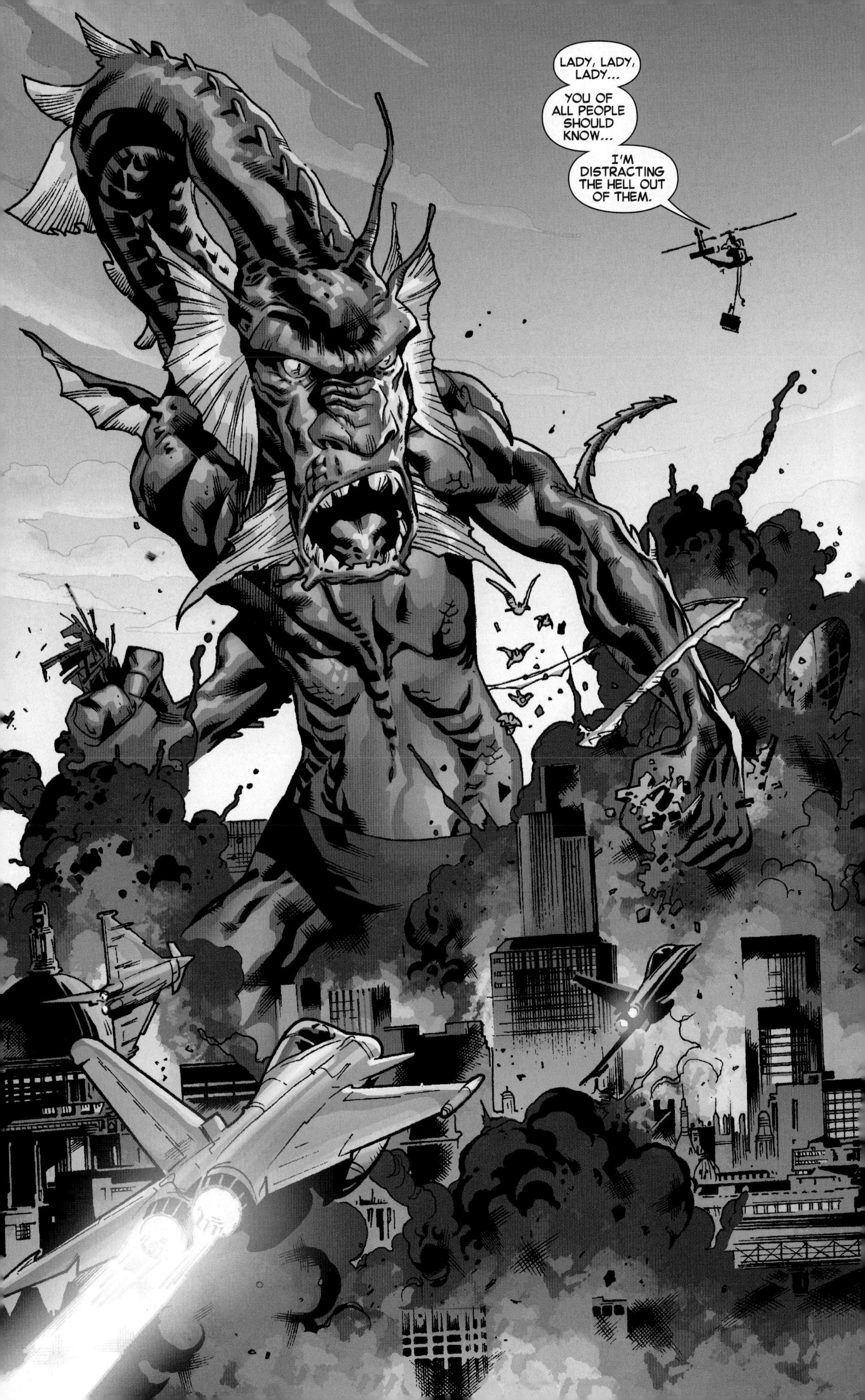
LADY, LADY, LADY...
YOU OF ALL PEOPLE SHOULD KNOW...
I'M DISTRACTING THE HELL OUT OF THEM.

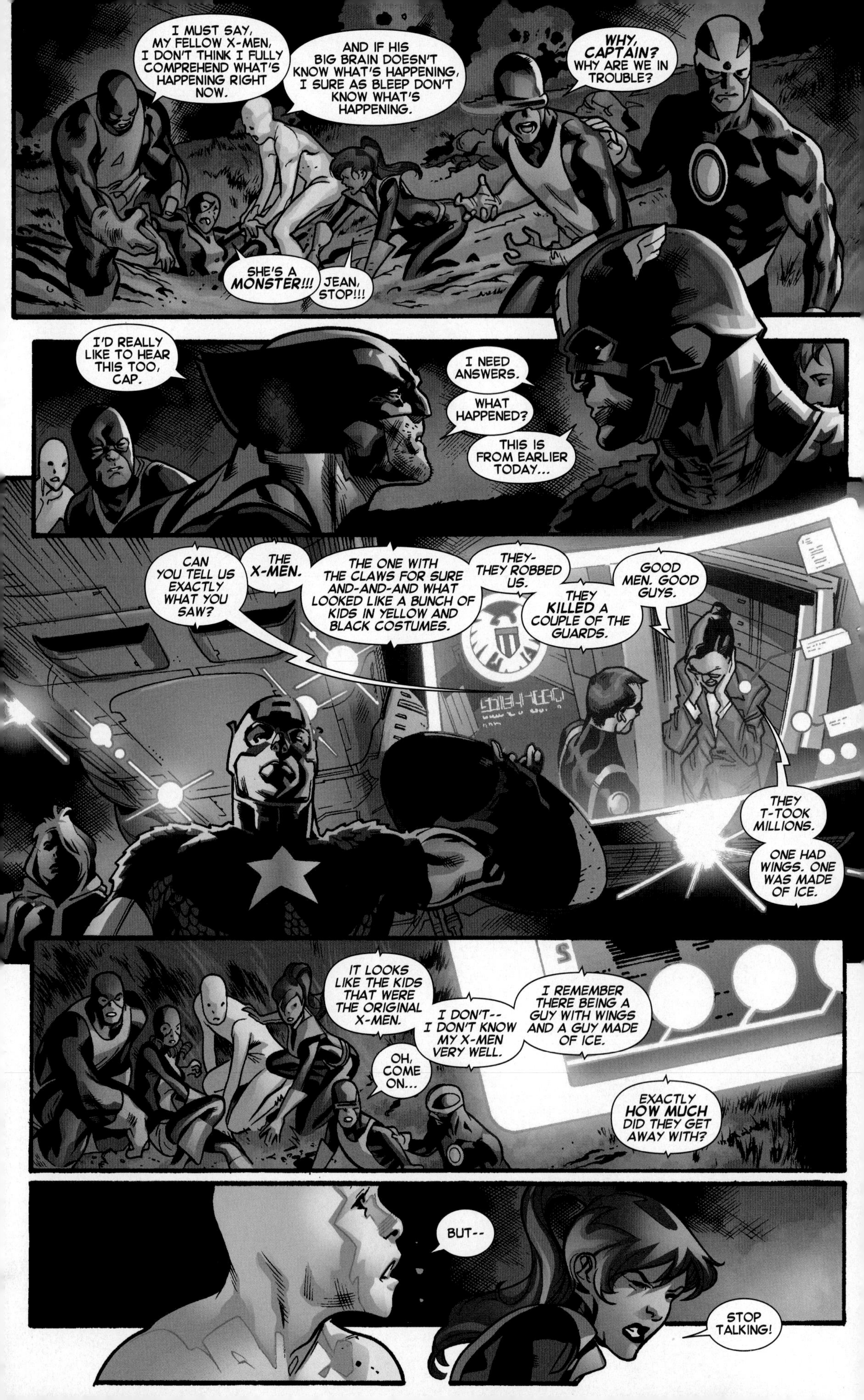
I MUST SAY, MY FELLOW X-MEN, I DON'T THINK I FULLY COMPREHEND WHAT'S HAPPENING RIGHT NOW.
AND IF HIS BIG BRAIN DOESN'T KNOW WHAT'S HAPPENING, I SURE AS BLEEP DON'T KNOW WHAT'S HAPPENING.
WHY, CAPTAIN? WHY ARE WE IN TROUBLE?
SHE'S A MONSTER!!!
JEAN, STOP!!!
I'D REALLY LIKE TO HEAR THIS TOO, CAP.
I NEED ANSWERS.
WHAT HAPPENED?
THIS IS FROM EARLIER TODAY...
CAN YOU TELL US EXACTLY WHAT YOU SAW?
THE X-MEN.
THE ONE WITH THE CLAWS FOR SURE AND-AND-AND WHAT LOOKED LIKE A BUNCH OF KIDS IN YELLOW AND BLACK COSTUMES.
THEY- THEY ROBBED US.
THEY KILLED A COUPLE OF THE GUARDS.
GOOD MEN. GOOD GUYS.
THEY T-TOOK MILLIONS.
ONE HAD WINGS. ONE WAS MADE OF ICE.
IT LOOKS LIKE THE KIDS THAT WERE THE ORIGINAL X-MEN.
I DON'T-- I DON'T KNOW MY X-MEN VERY WELL.
I REMEMBER THERE BEING A GUY WITH WINGS AND A GUY MADE OF ICE.
OH, COME ON...
EXACTLY HOW MUCH DID THEY GET AWAY WITH?
BUT--
STOP TALKING!

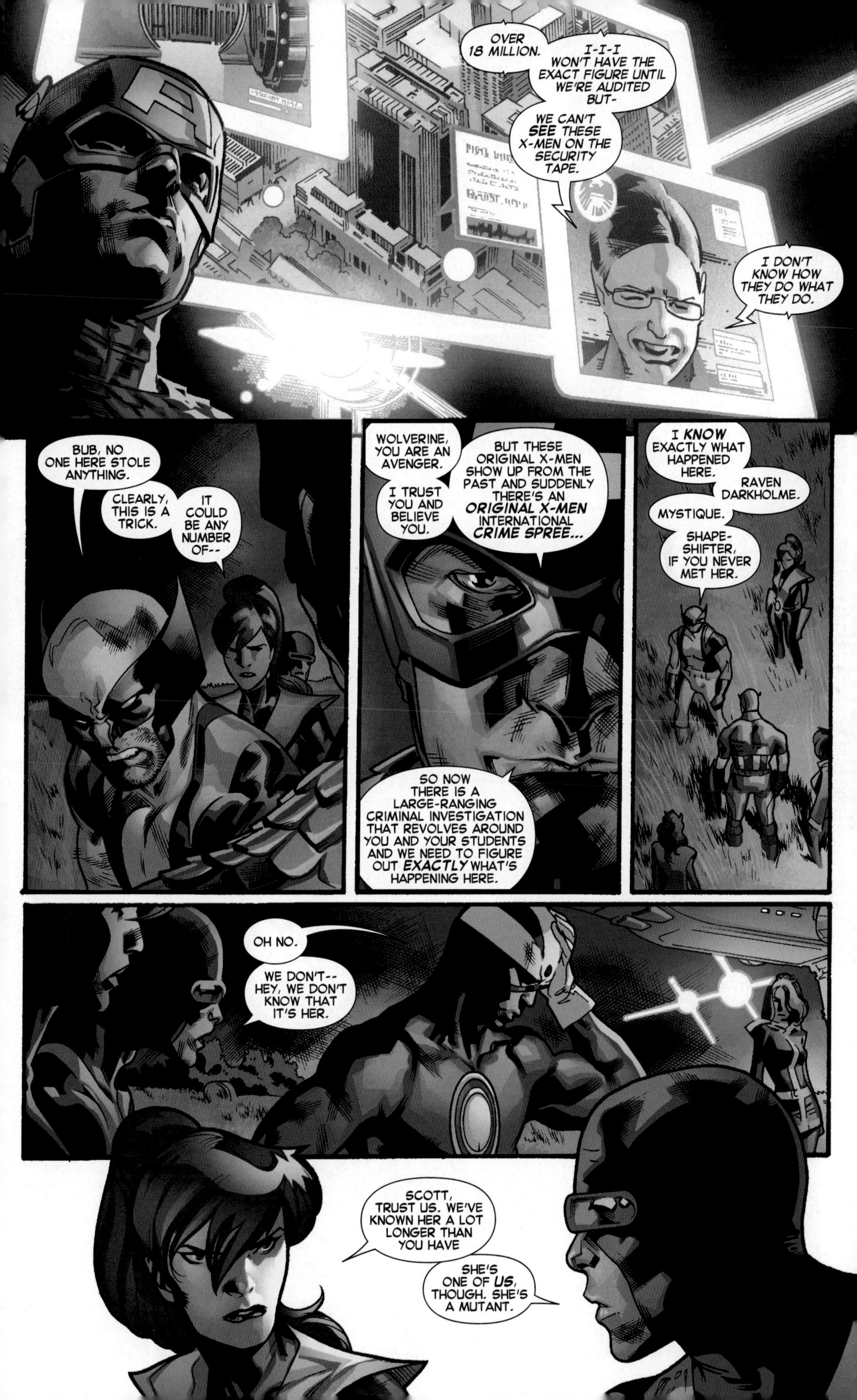
OVER 18 MILLION.
I-I-I WON'T HAVE THE EXACT FIGURE UNTIL WE'RE AUDITED BUT-
WE CAN'T SEE THESE X-MEN ON THE SECURITY TAPE.
I DON'T KNOW HOW THEY DO WHAT THEY DO.
BUB, NO ONE HERE STOLE ANYTHING.
CLEARLY, THIS IS A TRICK.
IT COULD BE ANY NUMBER OF--
WOLVERINE, YOU ARE AN AVENGER.
I TRUST YOU AND BELIEVE YOU.
BUT THESE ORIGINAL X-MEN SHOW UP FROM THE PAST AND SUDDENLY THERE'S AN ORIGINAL X-MEN INTERNATIONAL CRIME SPREE...
SO NOW THERE IS A LARGE-RANGING CRIMINAL INVESTIGATION THAT REVOLVES AROUND YOU AND YOUR STUDENTS AND WE NEED TO FIGURE OUT EXACTLY WHAT'S HAPPENING HERE.
I KNOW EXACTLY WHAT HAPPENED HERE.
RAVEN DARKHOLME.
MYSTIQUE.
SHAPE-SHIFTER, IF YOU NEVER MET HER.
OH NO.
WE DON'T-- HEY, WE DON'T KNOW THAT IT'S HER.
SCOTT, TRUST US. WE'VE KNOWN HER A LOT LONGER THAN YOU HAVE
SHE'S ONE OF US, THOUGH. SHE'S A MUTANT.

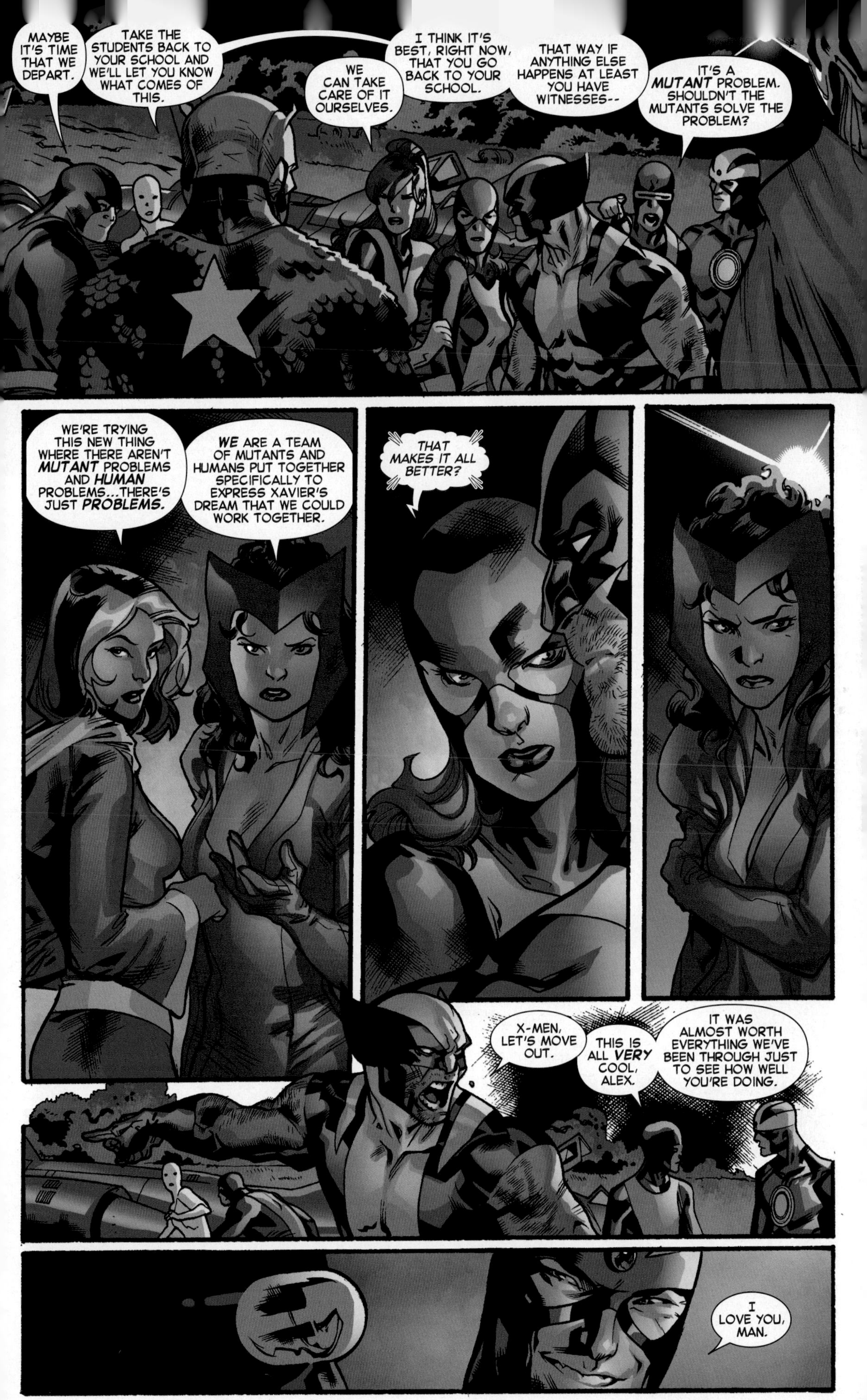
MAYBE IT'S TIME THAT WE DEPART.
TAKE THE STUDENTS BACK TO YOUR SCHOOL AND WE'LL LET YOU KNOW WHAT COMES OF THIS.
WE CAN TAKE CARE OF IT OURSELVES.
I THINK IT'S BEST, RIGHT NOW, THAT YOU GO BACK TO YOUR SCHOOL.
THAT WAY IF ANYTHING ELSE HAPPENS AT LEAST YOU HAVE WITNESSES--
IT'S A MUTANT PROBLEM. SHOULDN'T THE MUTANTS SOLVE THE PROBLEM?
WE'RE TRYING THIS NEW THING WHERE THERE AREN'T MUTANT PROBLEMS AND HUMAN PROBLEMS...THERE'S JUST PROBLEMS.
WE ARE A TEAM OF MUTANTS AND HUMANS PUT TOGETHER SPECIFICALLY TO EXPRESS XAVIER'S DREAM THAT WE COULD WORK TOGETHER.
THAT MAKES IT ALL BETTER?
X-MEN, LET'S MOVE OUT.
THIS IS ALL VERY COOL, ALEX.
IT WAS ALMOST WORTH EVERYTHING WE'VE BEEN THROUGH JUST TO SEE HOW WELL YOU'RE DOING.
I LOVE YOU, MAN.

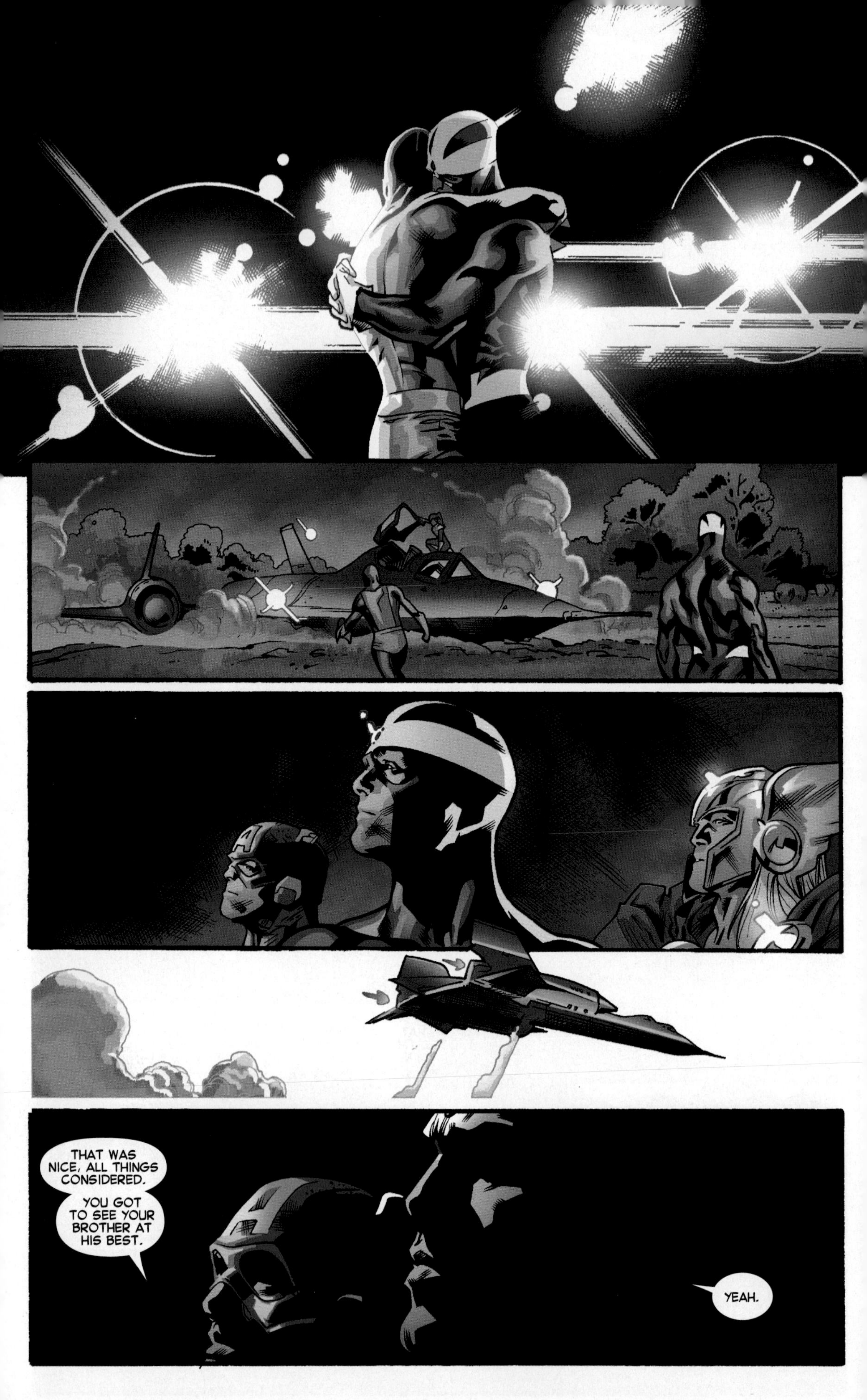
THAT WAS NICE, ALL THINGS CONSIDERED.
YOU GOT TO SEE YOUR BROTHER AT HIS BEST.
YEAH.

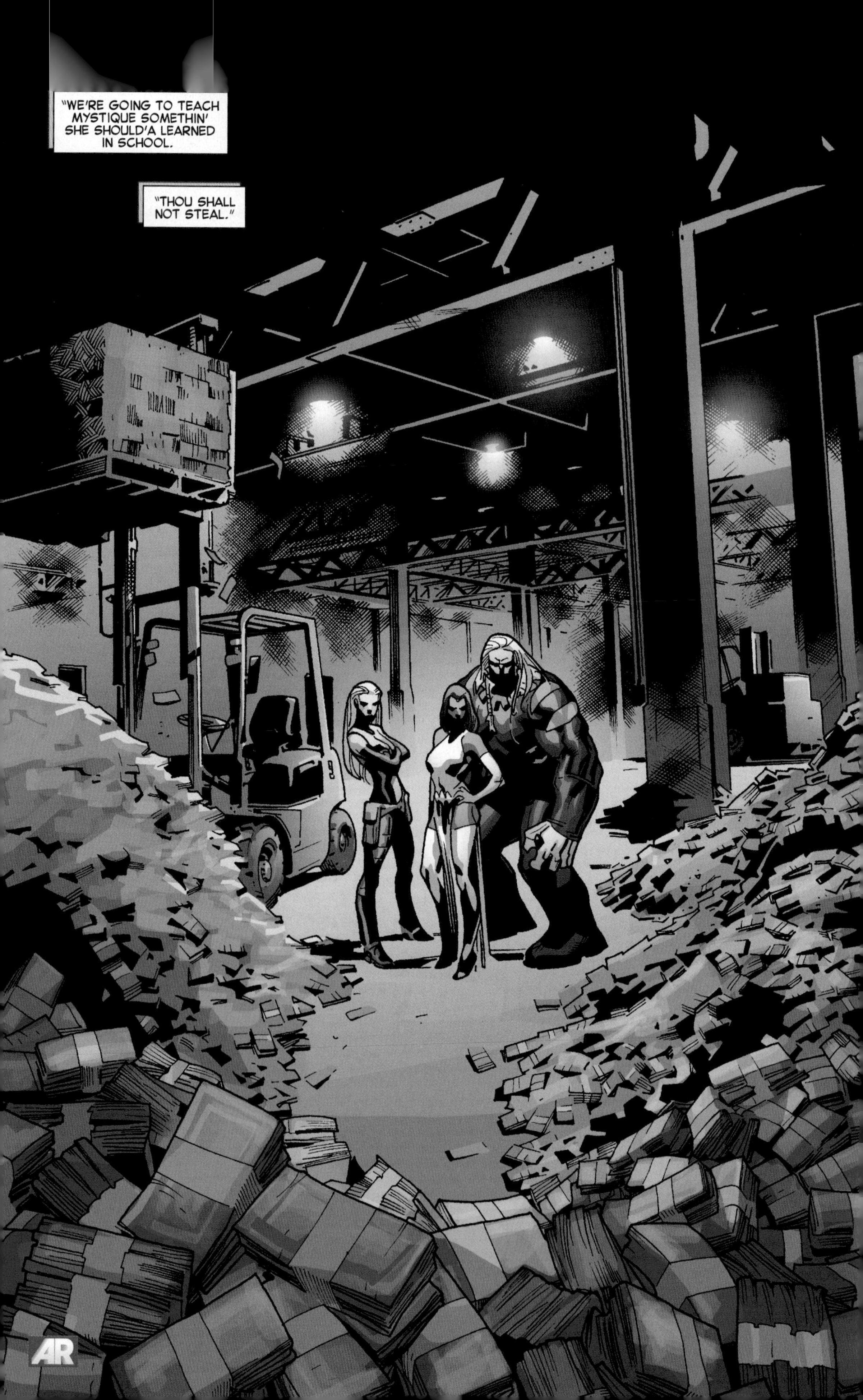
"WE'RE GOING TO TEACH MYSTIQUE SOMETHIN' SHE SHOULD'A LEARNED IN SCHOOL.
"THOU SHALL NOT STEAL."

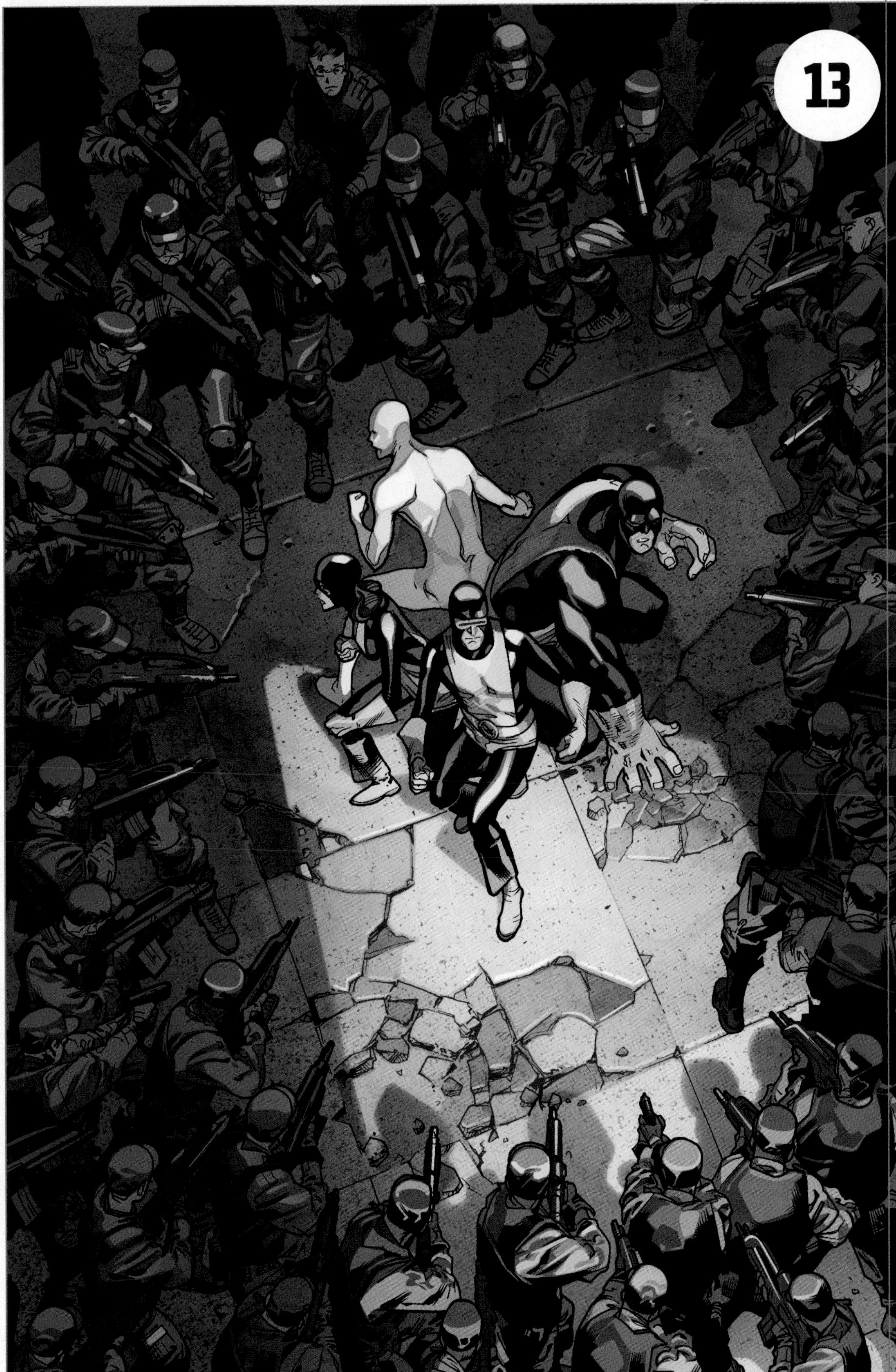
13

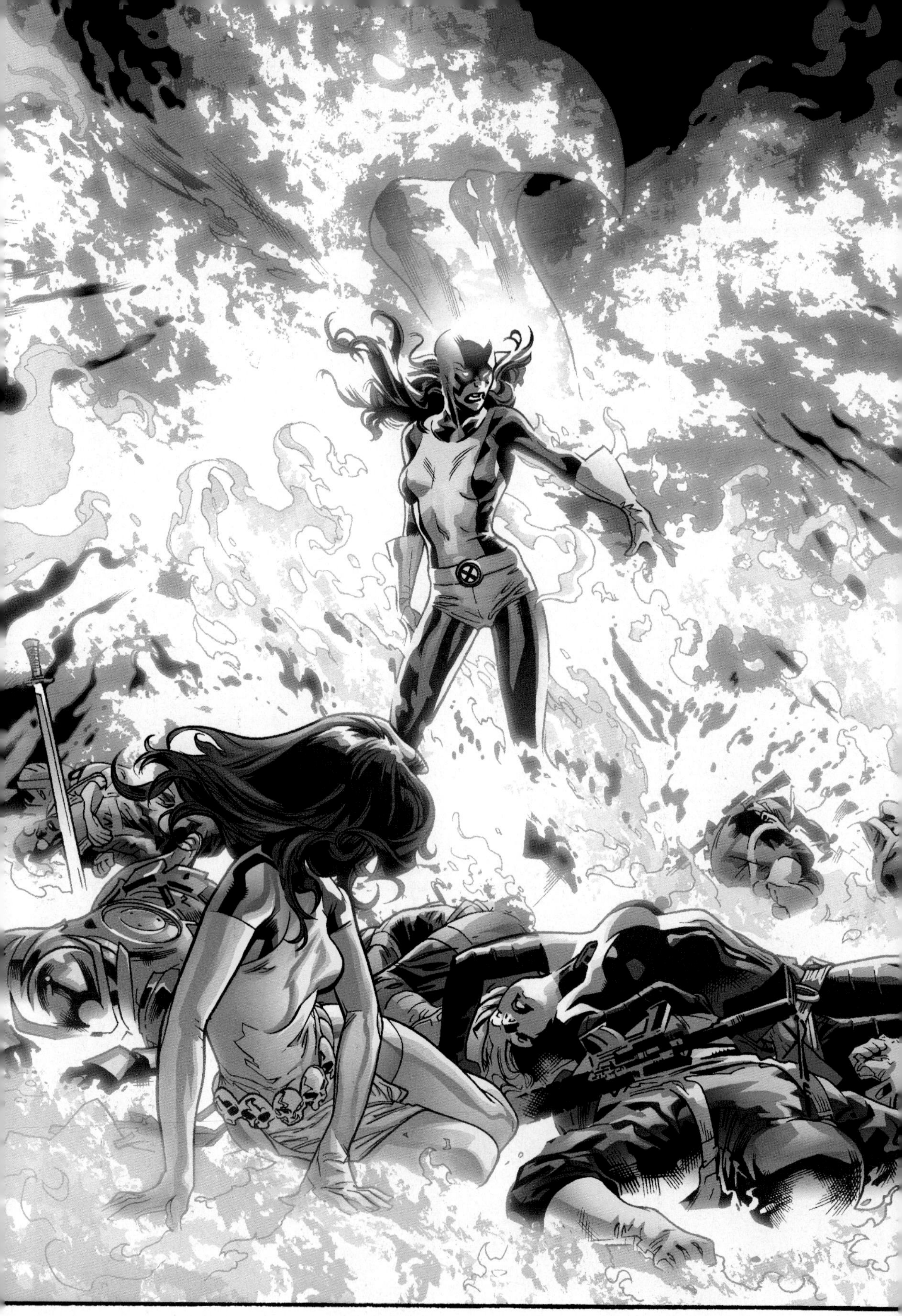

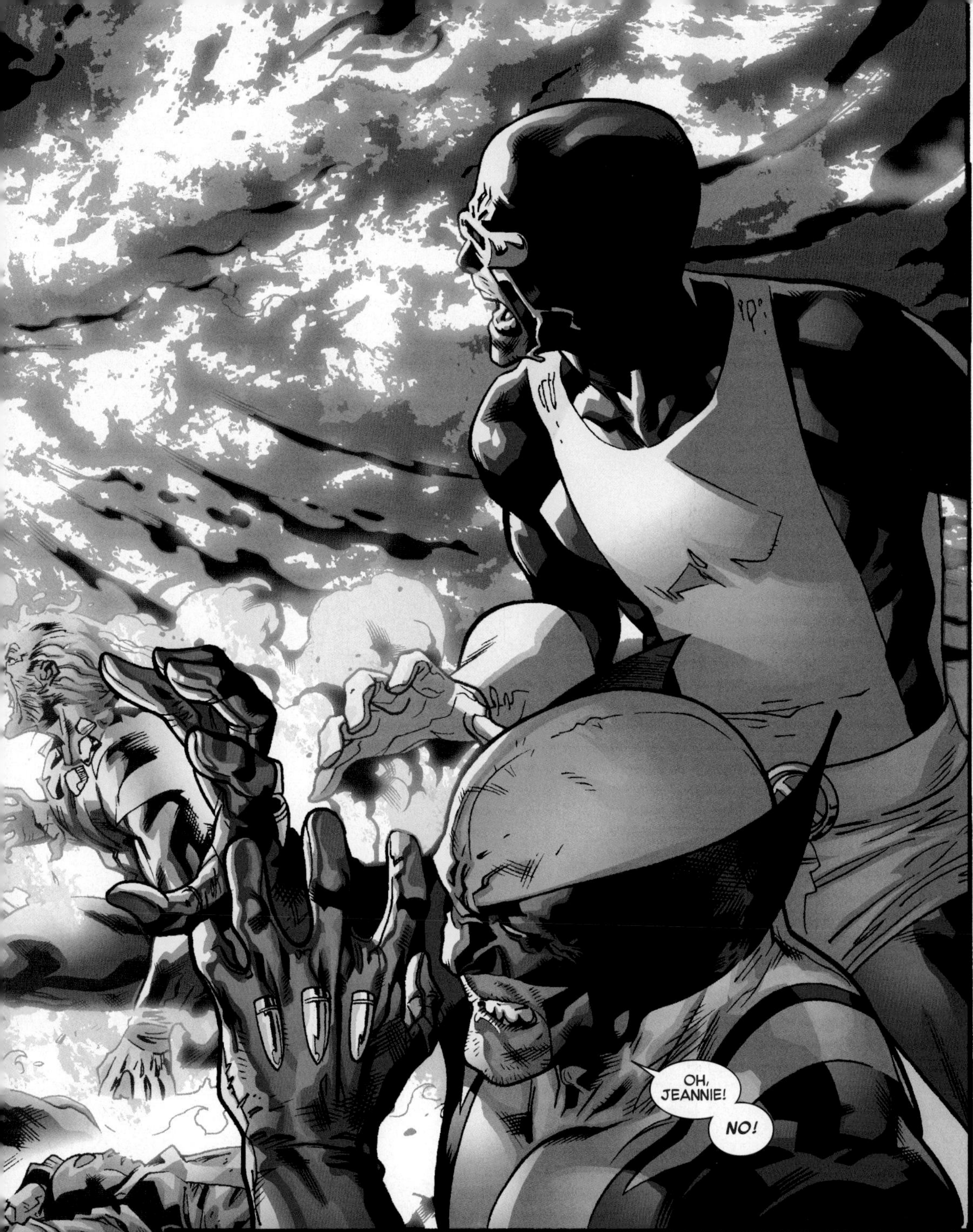
OH, JEANNIE!
NO!

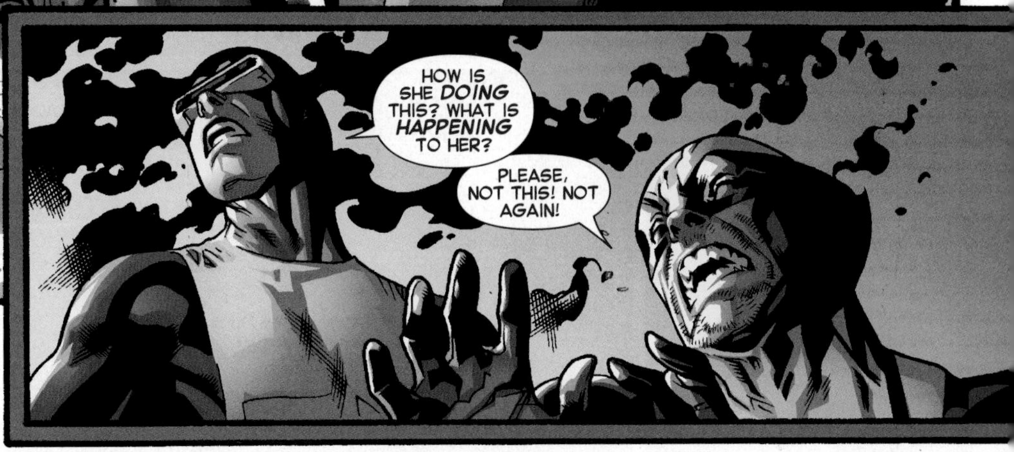
HOW IS SHE *DOING* THIS? WHAT IS *HAPPENING* TO HER?
PLEASE, NOT THIS! NOT AGAIN!

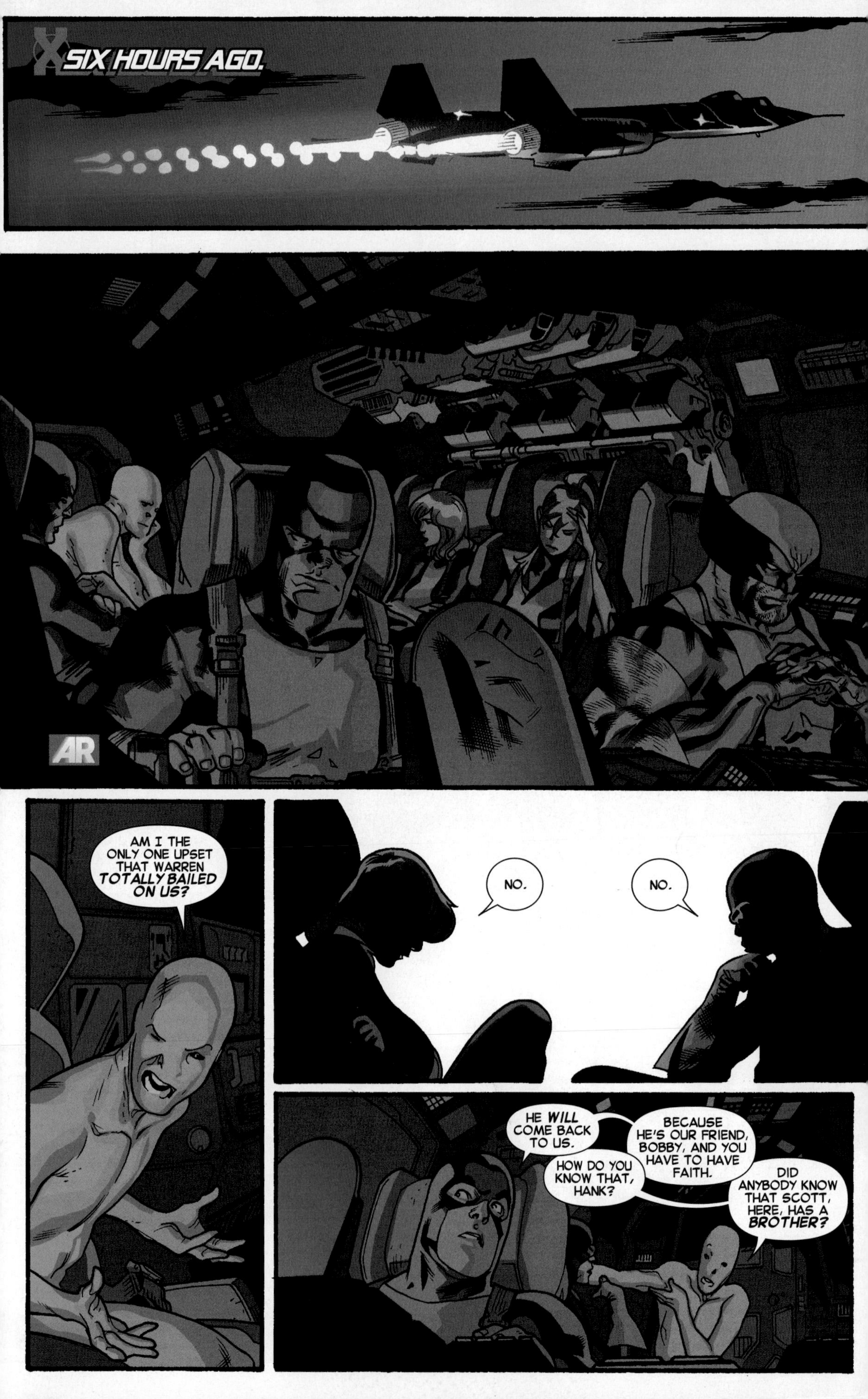
SIX HOURS AGO.
AR
AM I THE ONLY ONE UPSET THAT WARREN TOTALLY BAILED ON US?
NO.
NO.
HE WILL COME BACK TO US.
HOW DO YOU KNOW THAT, HANK?
BECAUSE HE'S OUR FRIEND, BOBBY, AND YOU HAVE TO HAVE FAITH.
DID ANYBODY KNOW THAT SCOTT, HERE, HAS A BROTHER?

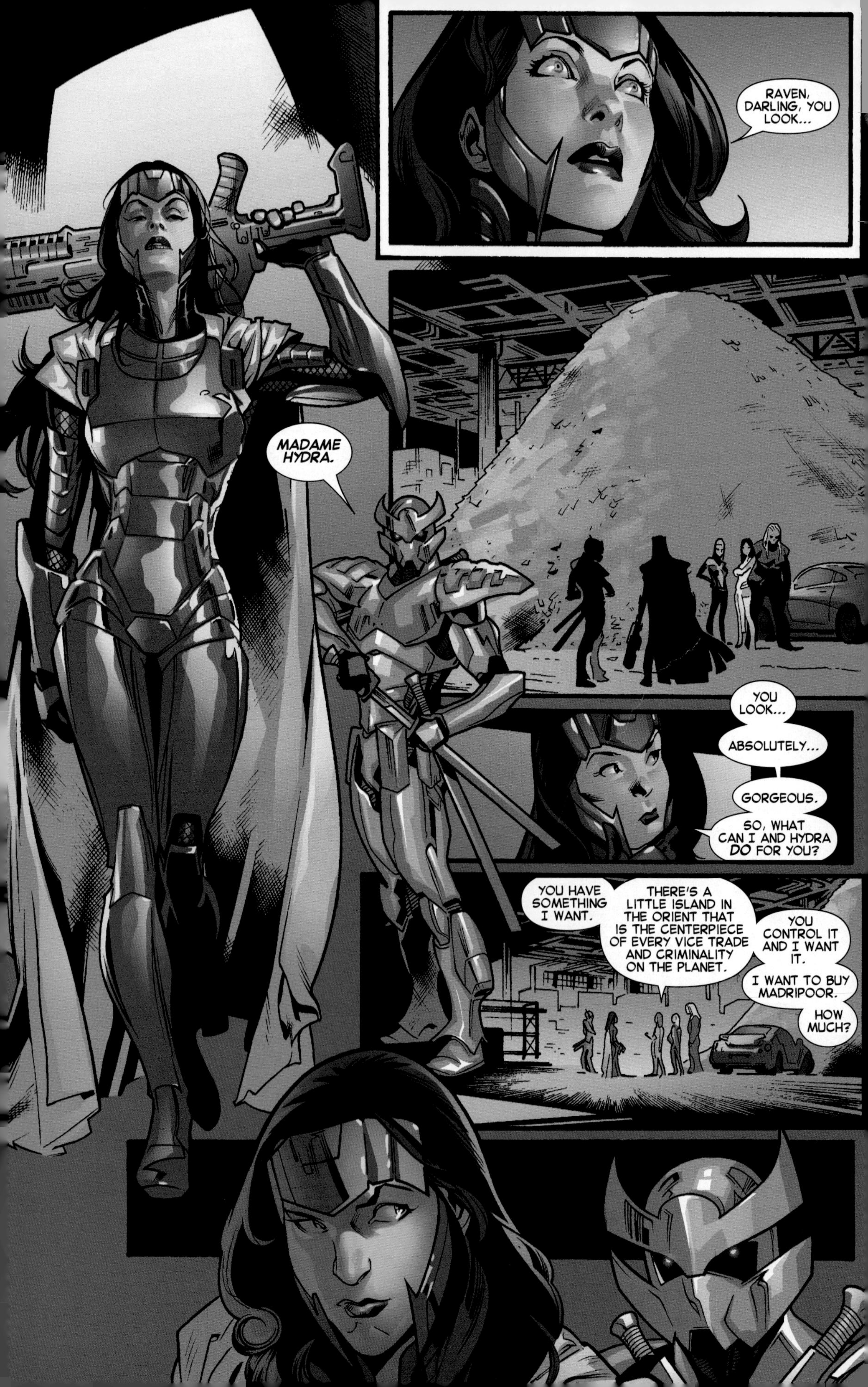
RAVEN, DARLING, YOU LOOK...
MADAME HYDRA.
YOU LOOK...
ABSOLUTELY...
GORGEOUS.
SO, WHAT CAN I AND HYDRA DO FOR YOU?
YOU HAVE SOMETHING I WANT.
THERE'S A LITTLE ISLAND IN THE ORIENT THAT IS THE CENTERPIECE OF EVERY VICE TRADE AND CRIMINALITY ON THE PLANET.
YOU CONTROL IT AND I WANT IT.
I WANT TO BUY MADRIPOOR.
HOW MUCH?

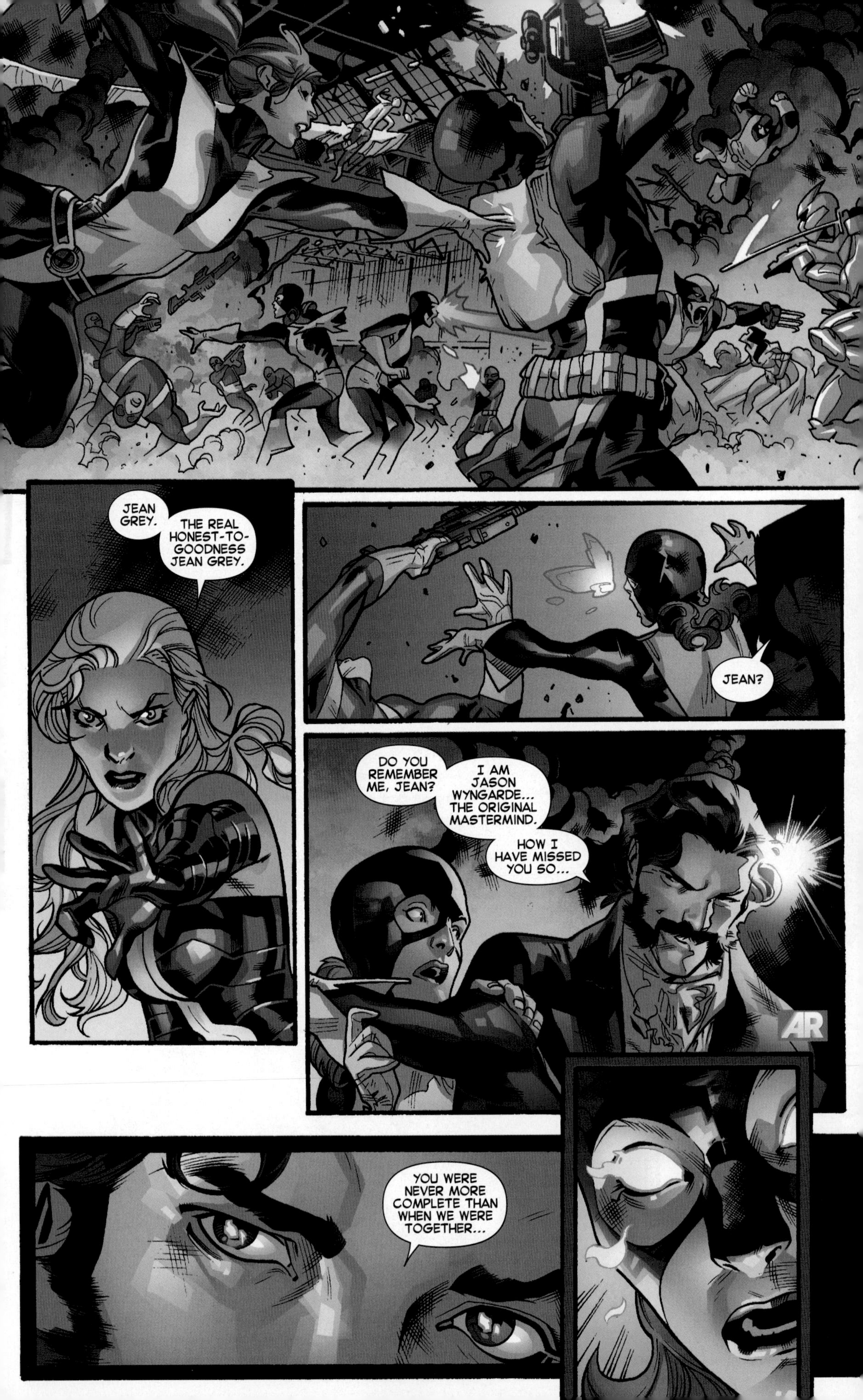
JEAN GREY.
THE REAL HONEST-TO-GOODNESS JEAN GREY.
JEAN?
DO YOU REMEMBER ME, JEAN?
I AM JASON WYNGARDE... THE ORIGINAL MASTERMIND.
HOW I HAVE MISSED YOU SO...
YOU WERE NEVER MORE COMPLETE THAN WHEN WE WERE TOGETHER...

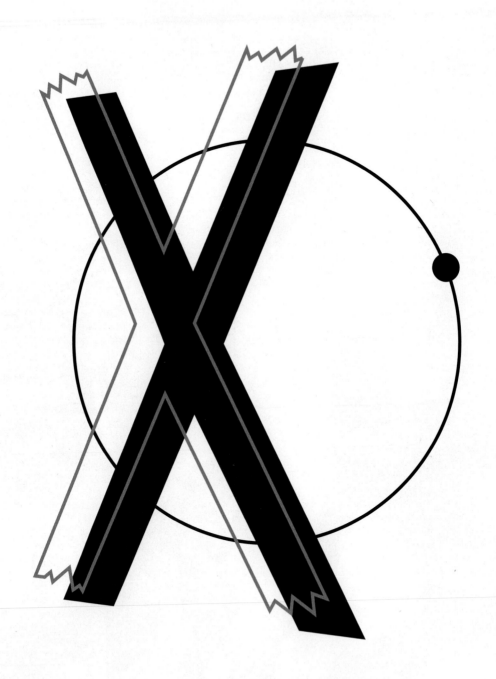

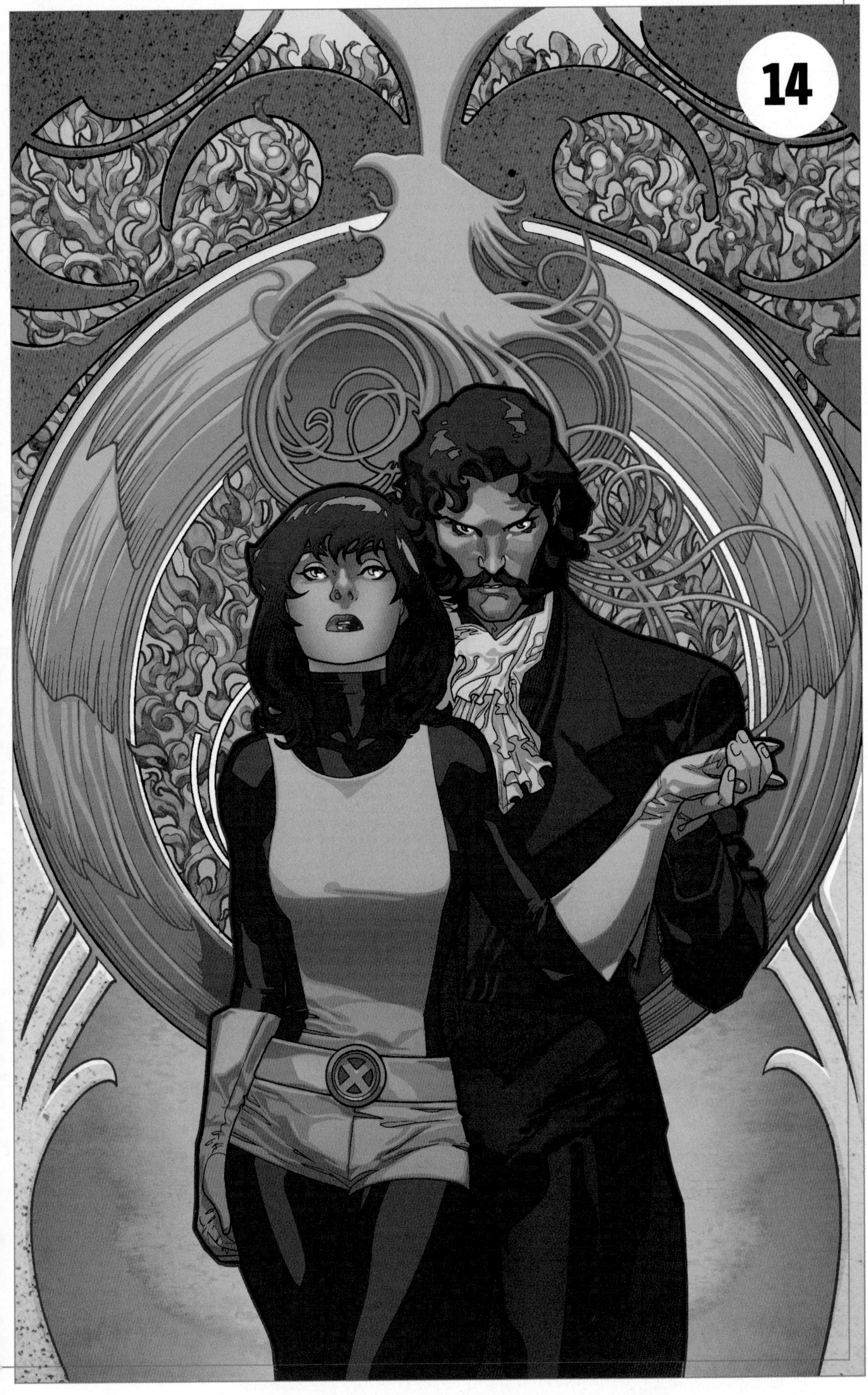
14

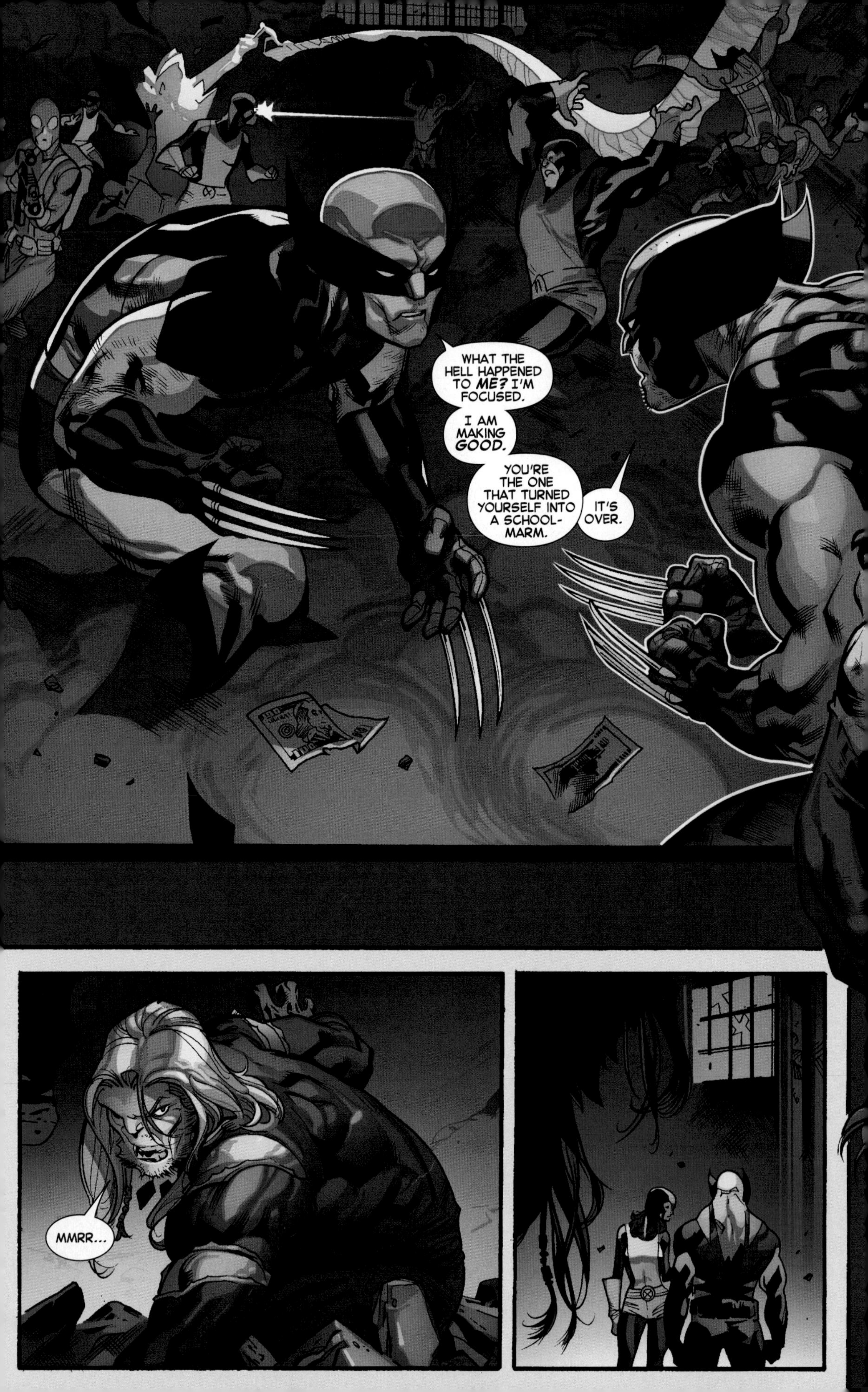
WHAT THE HELL HAPPENED TO ME? I'M FOCUSED.
I AM MAKING GOOD.
YOU'RE THE ONE THAT TURNED YOURSELF INTO A SCHOOL-MARM.
IT'S OVER.
MMRR...

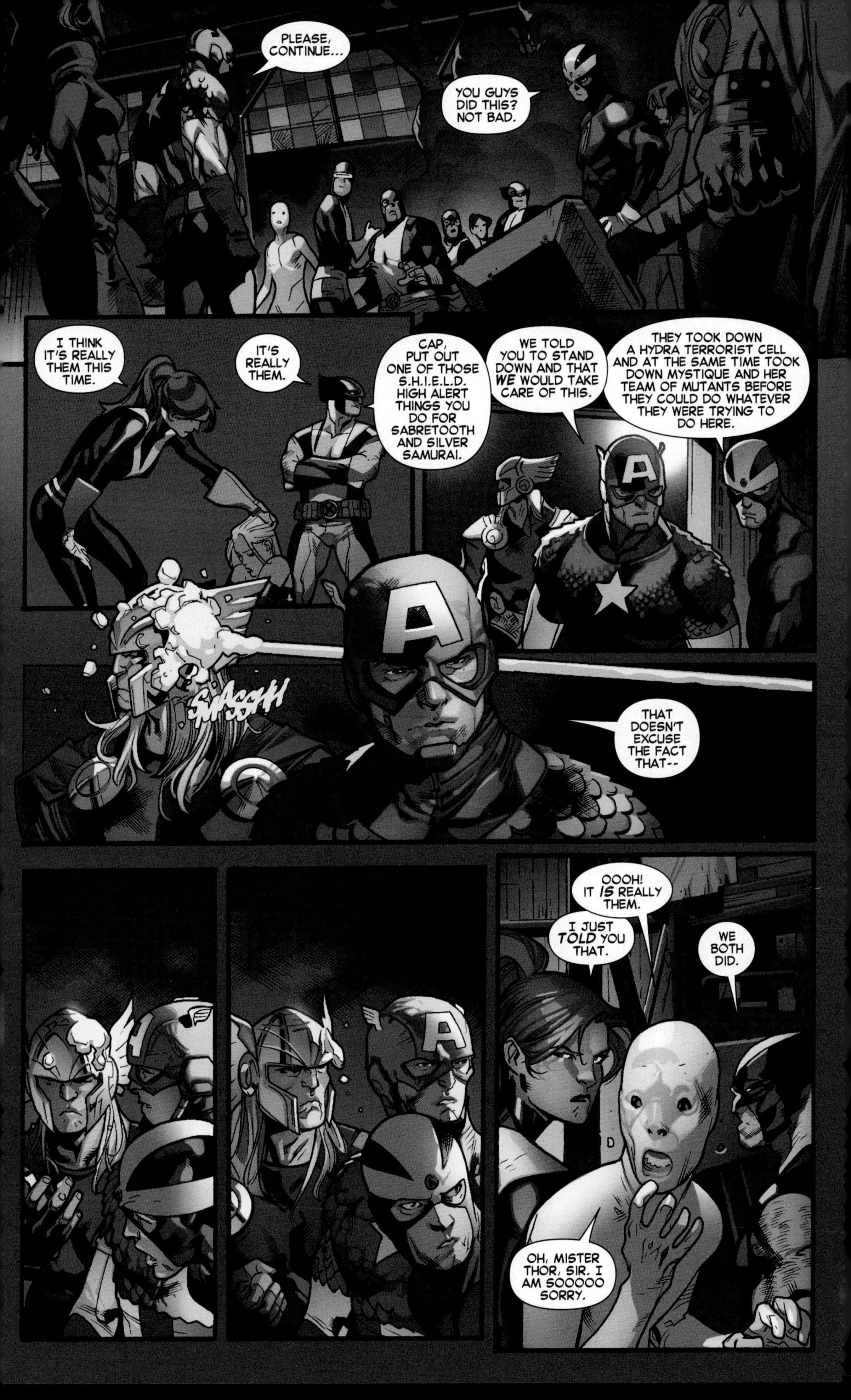
PLEASE, CONTINUE...
YOU GUYS DID THIS? NOT BAD.
I THINK IT'S REALLY THEM THIS TIME.
IT'S REALLY THEM.
CAP, PUT OUT ONE OF THOSE S.H.I.E.L.D. HIGH ALERT THINGS YOU DO FOR SABRETOOTH AND SILVER SAMURAI.
WE TOLD YOU TO STAND DOWN AND THAT WE WOULD TAKE CARE OF THIS.
THEY TOOK DOWN A HYDRA TERRORIST CELL AND AT THE SAME TIME TOOK DOWN MYSTIQUE AND HER TEAM OF MUTANTS BEFORE THEY COULD DO WHATEVER THEY WERE TRYING TO DO HERE.
SMASSHH
THAT DOESN'T EXCUSE THE FACT THAT--
OOOH! IT IS REALLY THEM.
I JUST TOLD YOU THAT.
WE BOTH DID.
OH, MISTER THOR, SIR. I AM SOOOOO SORRY.

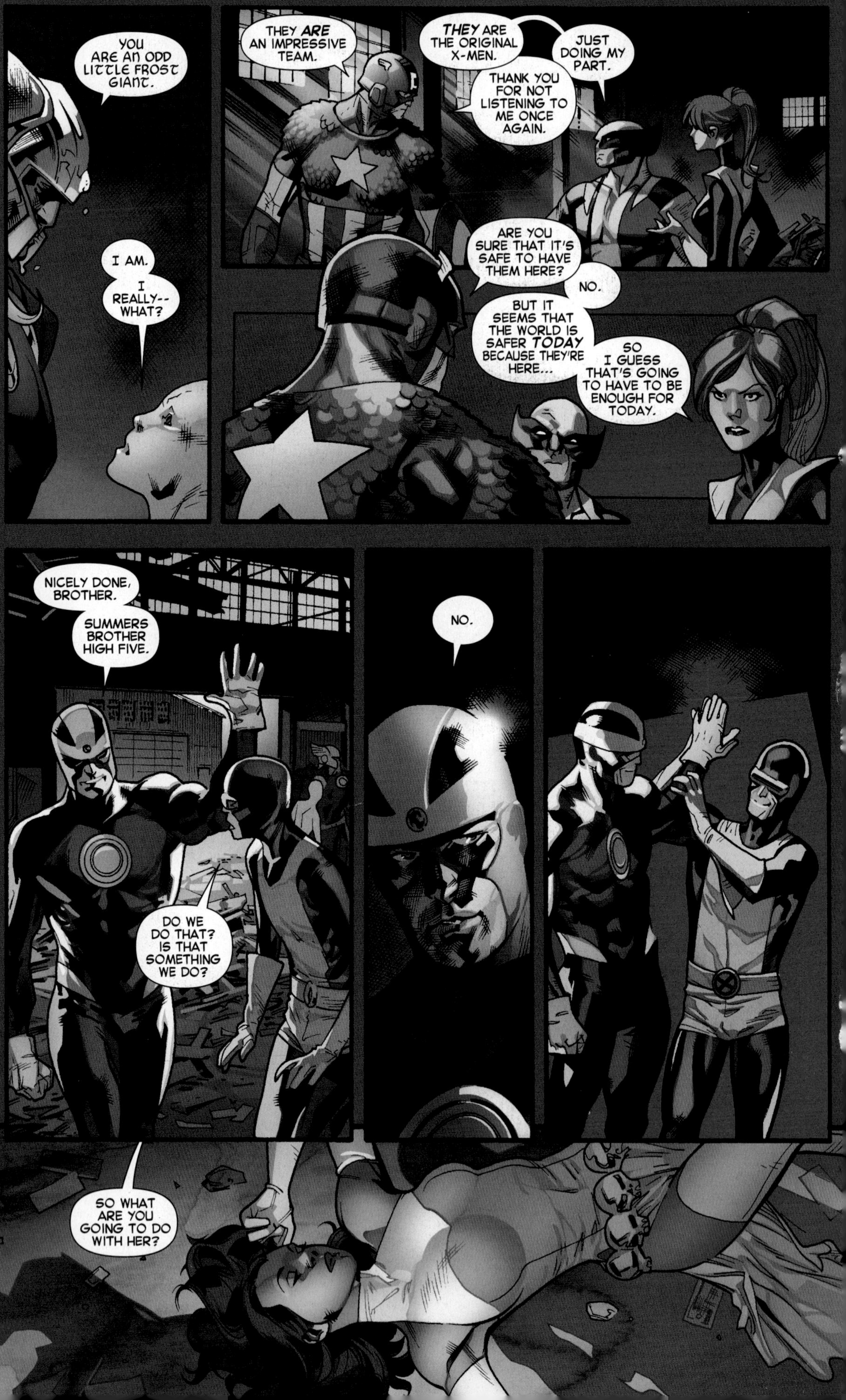
YOU ARE AN ODD LITTLE FROST GIANT.
I AM.
I REALLY--WHAT?
THEY ARE AN IMPRESSIVE TEAM.
THEY ARE THE ORIGINAL X-MEN.
THANK YOU FOR NOT LISTENING TO ME ONCE AGAIN.
JUST DOING MY PART.
ARE YOU SURE THAT IT'S SAFE TO HAVE THEM HERE?
NO.
BUT IT SEEMS THAT THE WORLD IS SAFER TODAY BECAUSE THEY'RE HERE...
SO I GUESS THAT'S GOING TO HAVE TO BE ENOUGH FOR TODAY.
NICELY DONE, BROTHER.
SUMMERS BROTHER HIGH FIVE.
DO WE DO THAT? IS THAT SOMETHING WE DO?
NO.
SO WHAT ARE YOU GOING TO DO WITH HER?

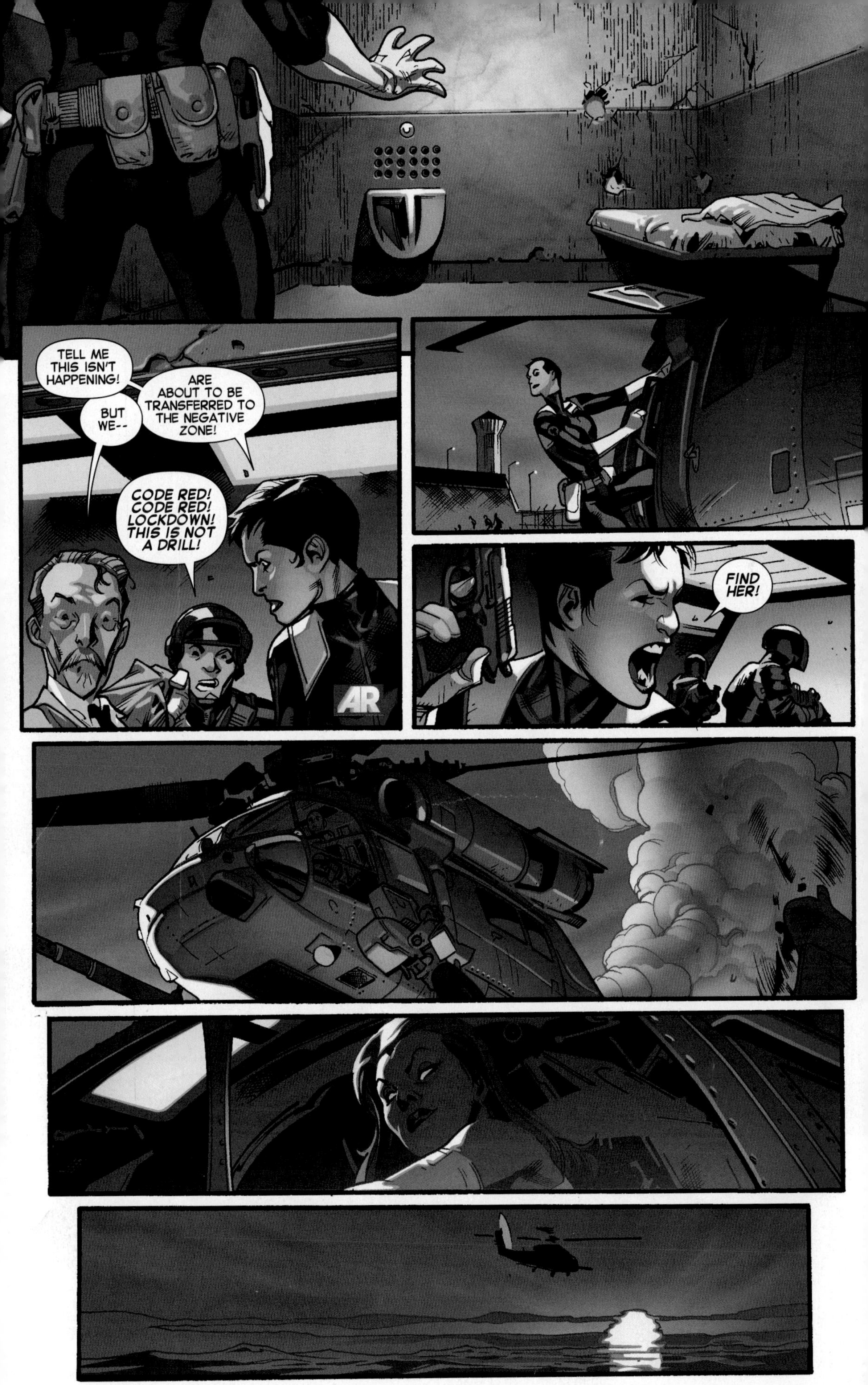
TELL ME THIS ISN'T HAPPENING!
BUT WE--
ARE ABOUT TO BE TRANSFERRED TO THE NEGATIVE ZONE!
CODE RED! CODE RED! LOCKDOWN! THIS IS NOT A DRILL!
FIND HER!

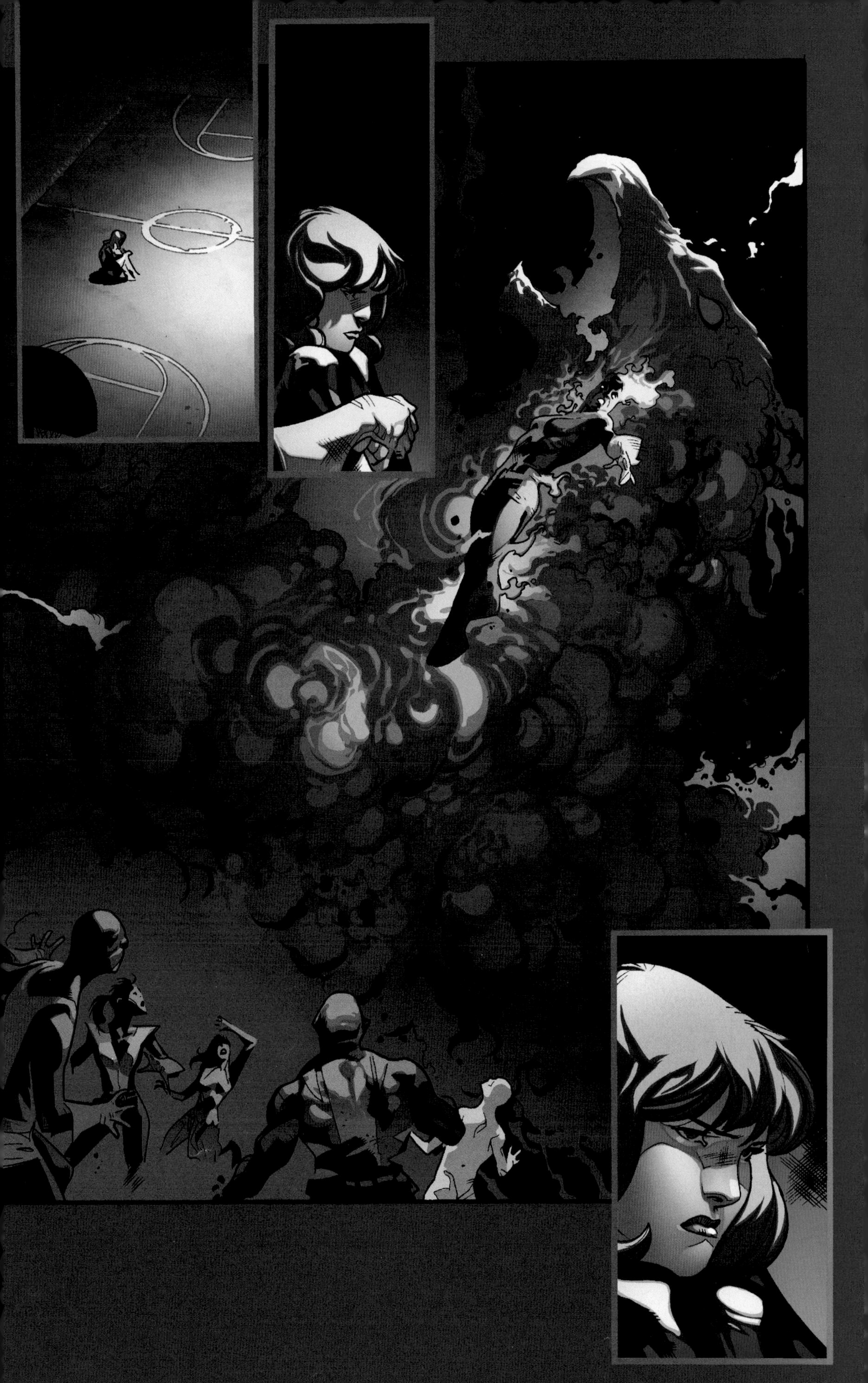

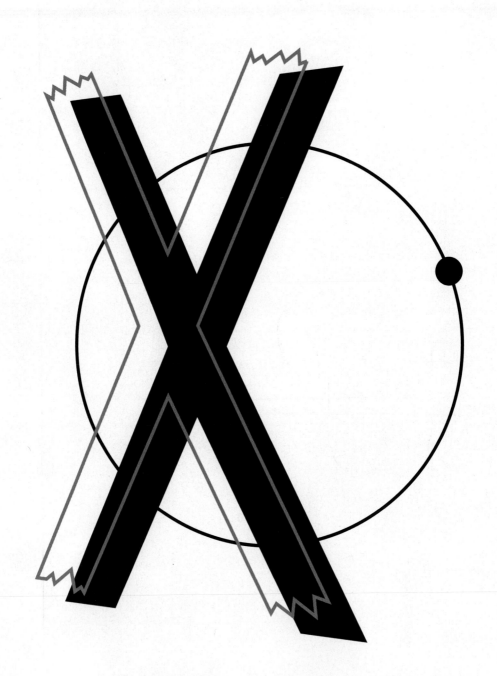

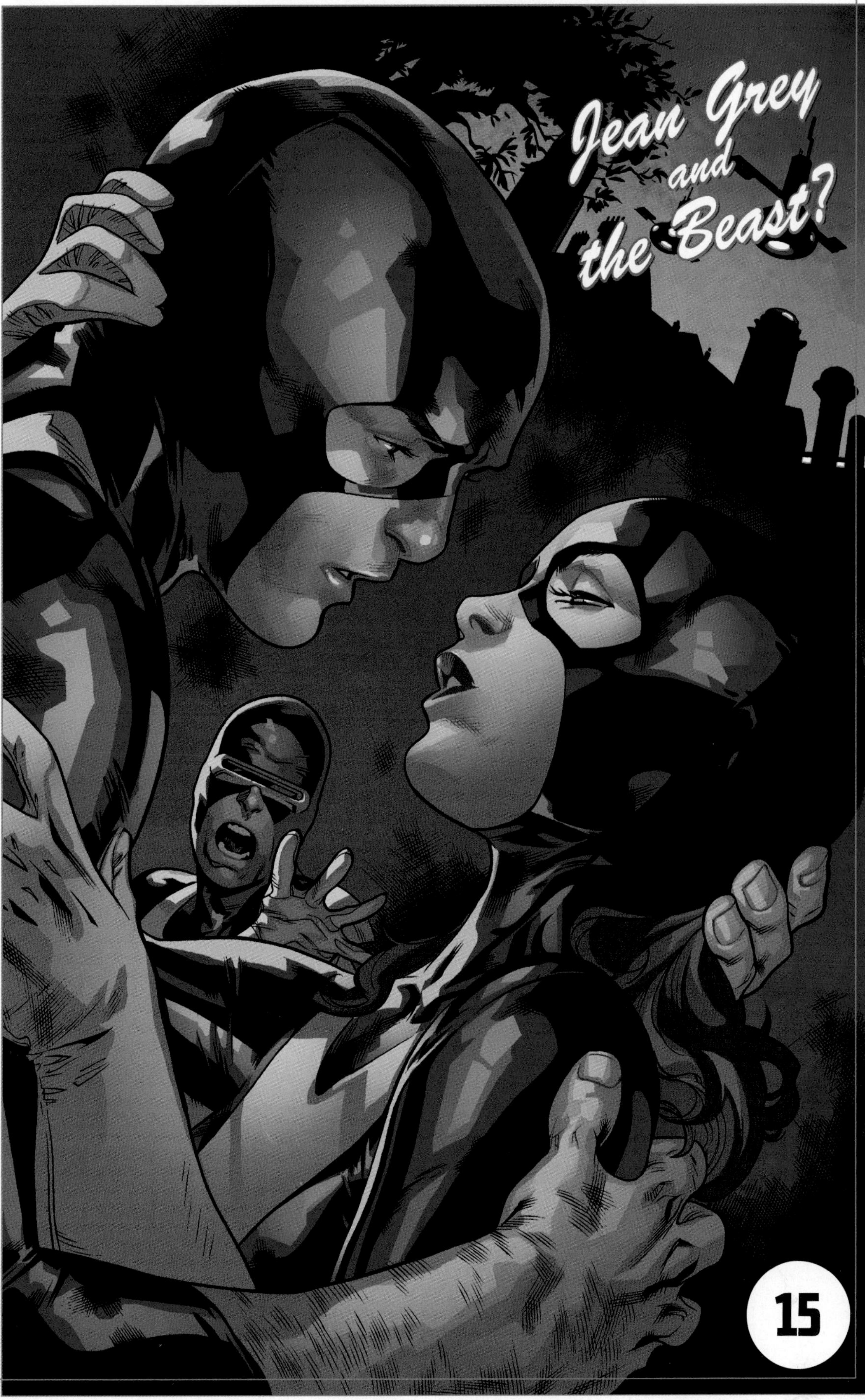
Jean Grey and the Beast?
15

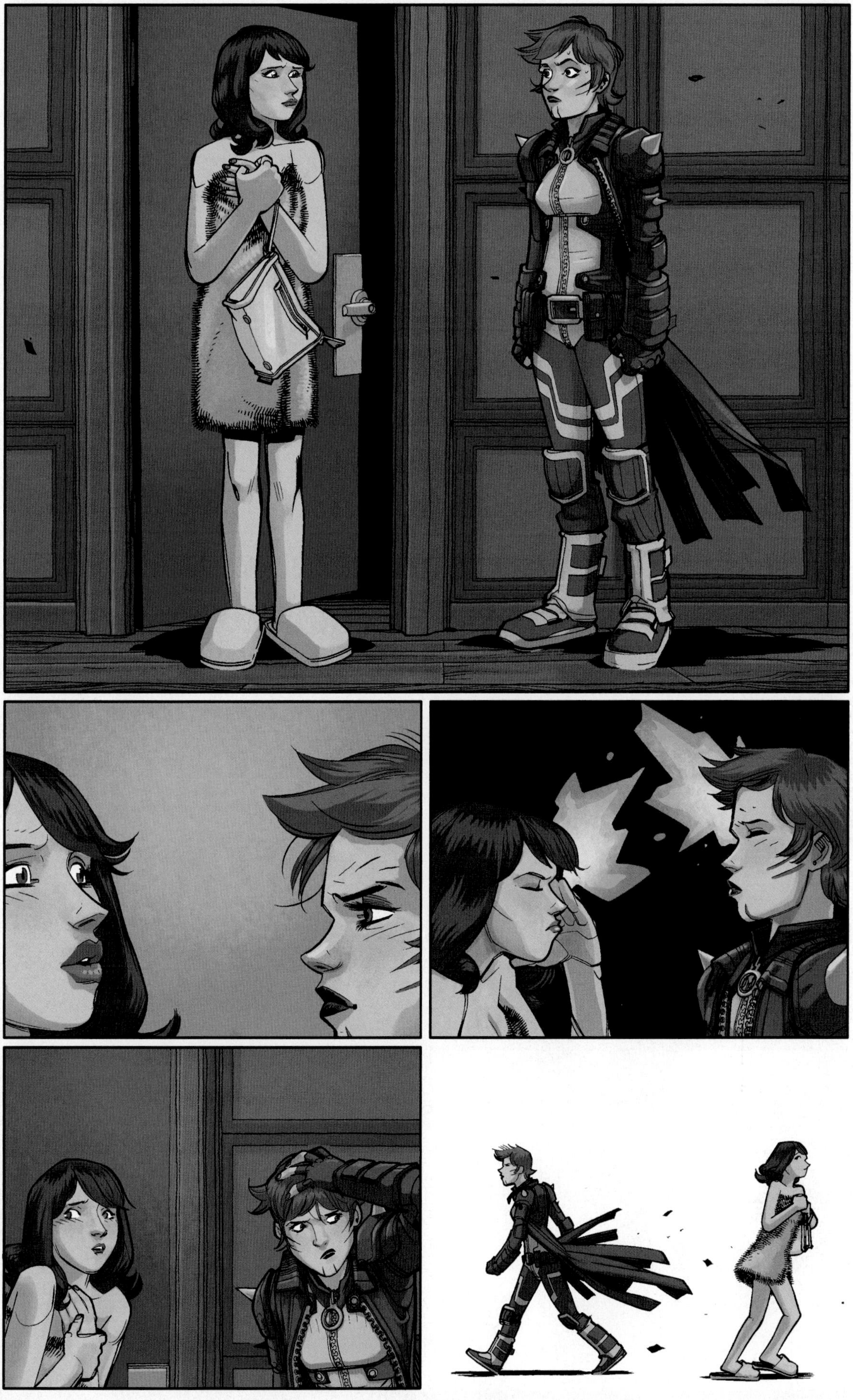

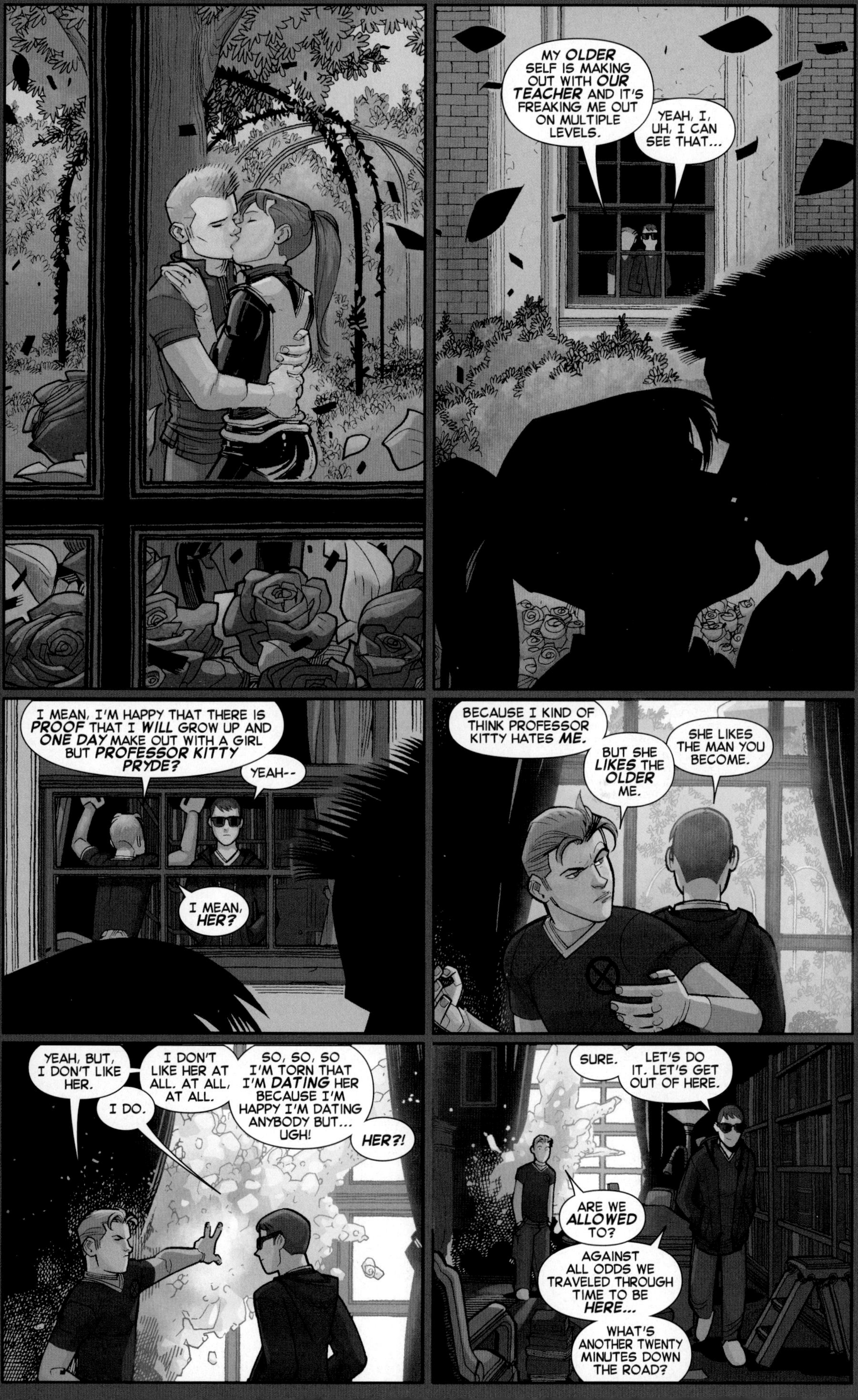
MY OLDER SELF IS MAKING OUT WITH OUR TEACHER AND IT'S FREAKING ME OUT ON MULTIPLE LEVELS.
YEAH, I, UH, I CAN SEE THAT...
I MEAN, I'M HAPPY THAT THERE IS PROOF THAT I WILL GROW UP AND ONE DAY MAKE OUT WITH A GIRL BUT PROFESSOR KITTY PRYDE?
YEAH--
I MEAN, HER?
BECAUSE I KIND OF THINK PROFESSOR KITTY HATES ME.
BUT SHE LIKES THE OLDER ME.
SHE LIKES THE MAN YOU BECOME.
YEAH, BUT, I DON'T LIKE HER.
I DO.
I DON'T LIKE HER AT ALL. AT ALL, AT ALL.
SO, SO, SO I'M TORN THAT I'M DATING HER BECAUSE I'M HAPPY I'M DATING ANYBODY BUT... UGH!
HER?!
SURE.
LET'S DO IT. LET'S GET OUT OF HERE.
ARE WE ALLOWED TO?
AGAINST ALL ODDS WE TRAVELED THROUGH TIME TO BE HERE...
WHAT'S ANOTHER TWENTY MINUTES DOWN THE ROAD?

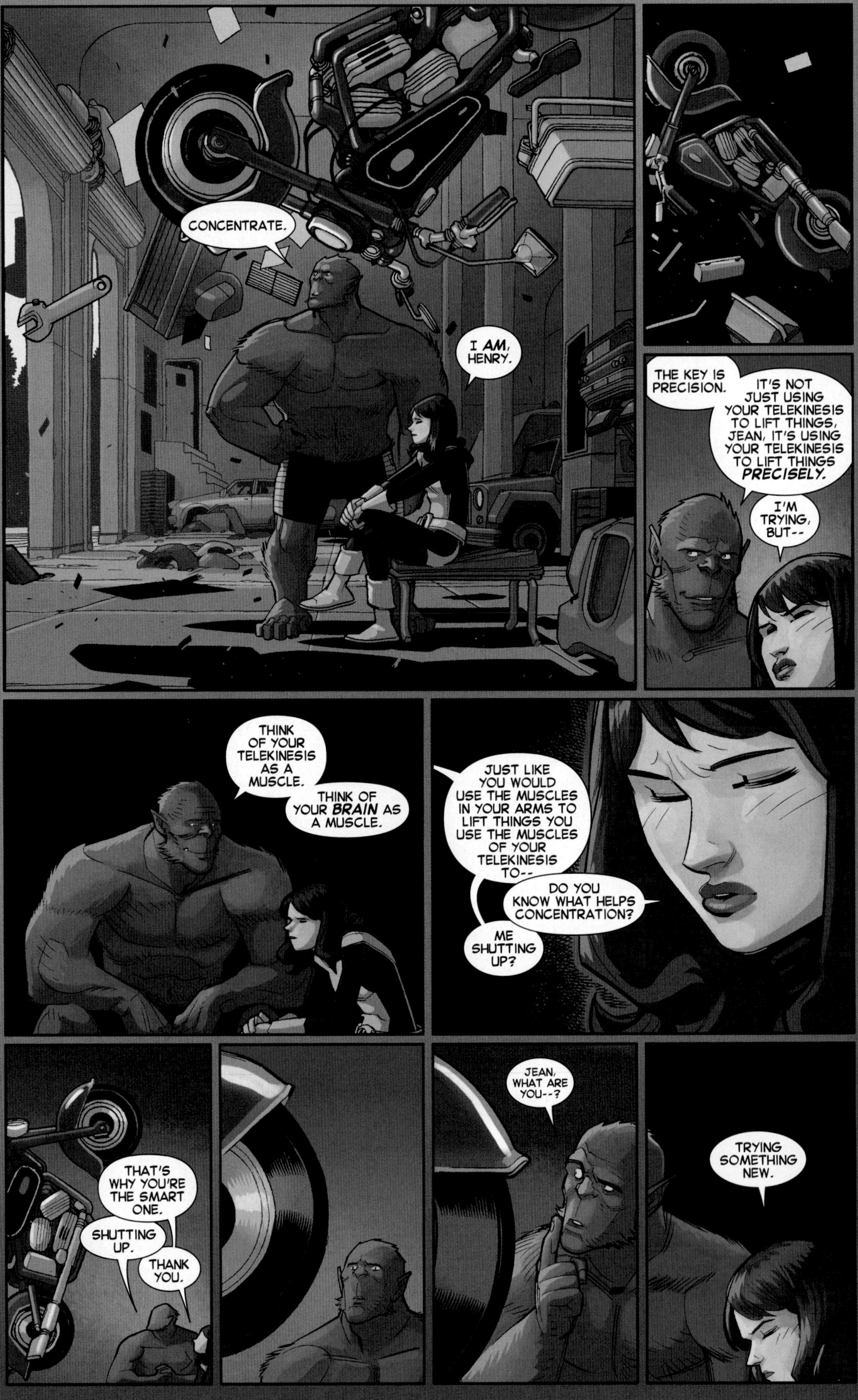
CONCENTRATE.
I AM, HENRY.
THE KEY IS PRECISION.
IT'S NOT JUST USING YOUR TELEKINESIS TO LIFT THINGS, JEAN, IT'S USING YOUR TELEKINESIS TO LIFT THINGS PRECISELY.
I'M TRYING, BUT--
THINK OF YOUR TELEKINESIS AS A MUSCLE.
THINK OF YOUR BRAIN AS A MUSCLE.
JUST LIKE YOU WOULD USE THE MUSCLES IN YOUR ARMS TO LIFT THINGS YOU USE THE MUSCLES OF YOUR TELEKINESIS TO--
DO YOU KNOW WHAT HELPS CONCENTRATION?
ME SHUTTING UP?
THAT'S WHY YOU'RE THE SMART ONE.
SHUTTING UP.
THANK YOU.
JEAN, WHAT ARE YOU--?
TRYING SOMETHING NEW.

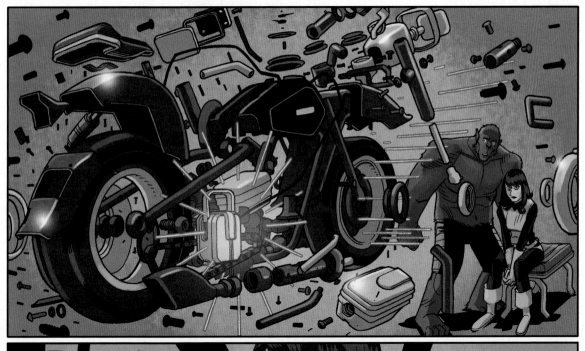

THAT *IS* IMPRESSIVE.

I AM COMPLETELY SCARED TO OPEN MY EYES BECAUSE I DON'T WANT TO LOSE--

VRRROOOOOMMMMM

CONCENTRATION.

HEY, FOXY LADY!

WE'LL BE BACK TO PICK YOU UP LATER!

HEY!

NOT REALLY!

CRUNKLE

CRAASH

DAMN!

CLONK

CLANG

HEY!!!

THAT'S MY JEEP!

WHY ARE YOU PEOPLE ALWAYS STEALING MY--?!

THINGS.

LOGAN--

THAT'S MY MOTORCYCLE, HANK.

LOGAN, IT WAS--

THAT'S MY MOTORCYCLE, HANK.

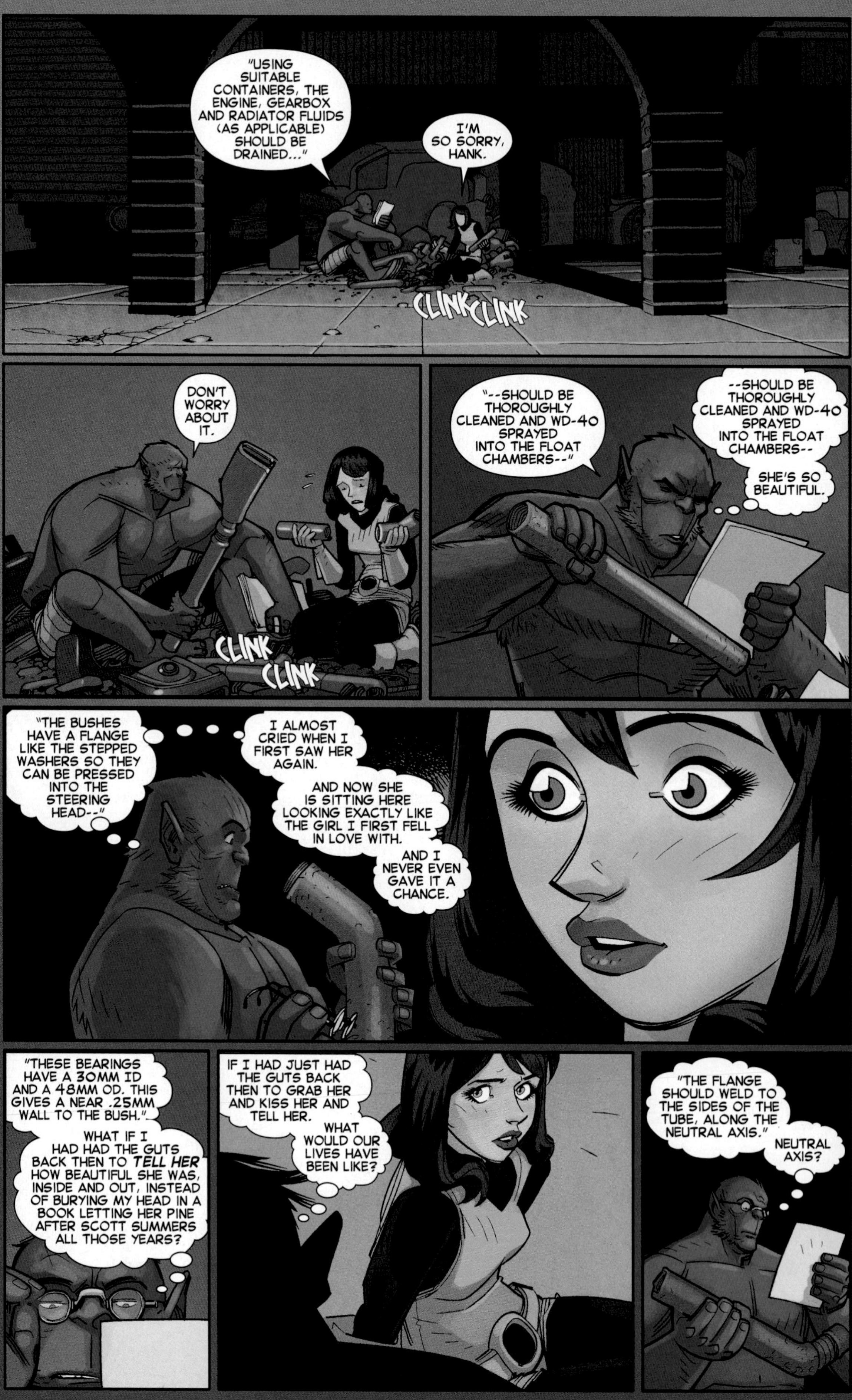
"USING SUITABLE CONTAINERS, THE ENGINE, GEARBOX AND RADIATOR FLUIDS (AS APPLICABLE) SHOULD BE DRAINED..."
I'M SO SORRY, HANK.
CLINK CLINK
DON'T WORRY ABOUT IT.
CLINK
CLINK
"--SHOULD BE THOROUGHLY CLEANED AND WD-40 SPRAYED INTO THE FLOAT CHAMBERS--"
--SHOULD BE THOROUGHLY CLEANED AND WD-40 SPRAYED INTO THE FLOAT CHAMBERS--
SHE'S SO BEAUTIFUL.
"THE BUSHES HAVE A FLANGE LIKE THE STEPPED WASHERS SO THEY CAN BE PRESSED INTO THE STEERING HEAD--"
I ALMOST CRIED WHEN I FIRST SAW HER AGAIN.
AND NOW SHE IS SITTING HERE LOOKING EXACTLY LIKE THE GIRL I FIRST FELL IN LOVE WITH.
AND I NEVER EVEN GAVE IT A CHANCE.
"THESE BEARINGS HAVE A 30MM ID AND A 48MM OD. THIS GIVES A NEAR .25MM WALL TO THE BUSH."
WHAT IF I HAD HAD THE GUTS BACK THEN TO *TELL HER* HOW BEAUTIFUL SHE WAS, INSIDE AND OUT, INSTEAD OF BURYING MY HEAD IN A BOOK LETTING HER PINE AFTER SCOTT SUMMERS ALL THOSE YEARS?
IF I HAD JUST HAD THE GUTS BACK THEN TO GRAB HER AND KISS HER AND TELL HER.
WHAT WOULD OUR LIVES HAVE BEEN LIKE?
"THE FLANGE SHOULD WELD TO THE SIDES OF THE TUBE, ALONG THE NEUTRAL AXIS."
NEUTRAL AXIS?

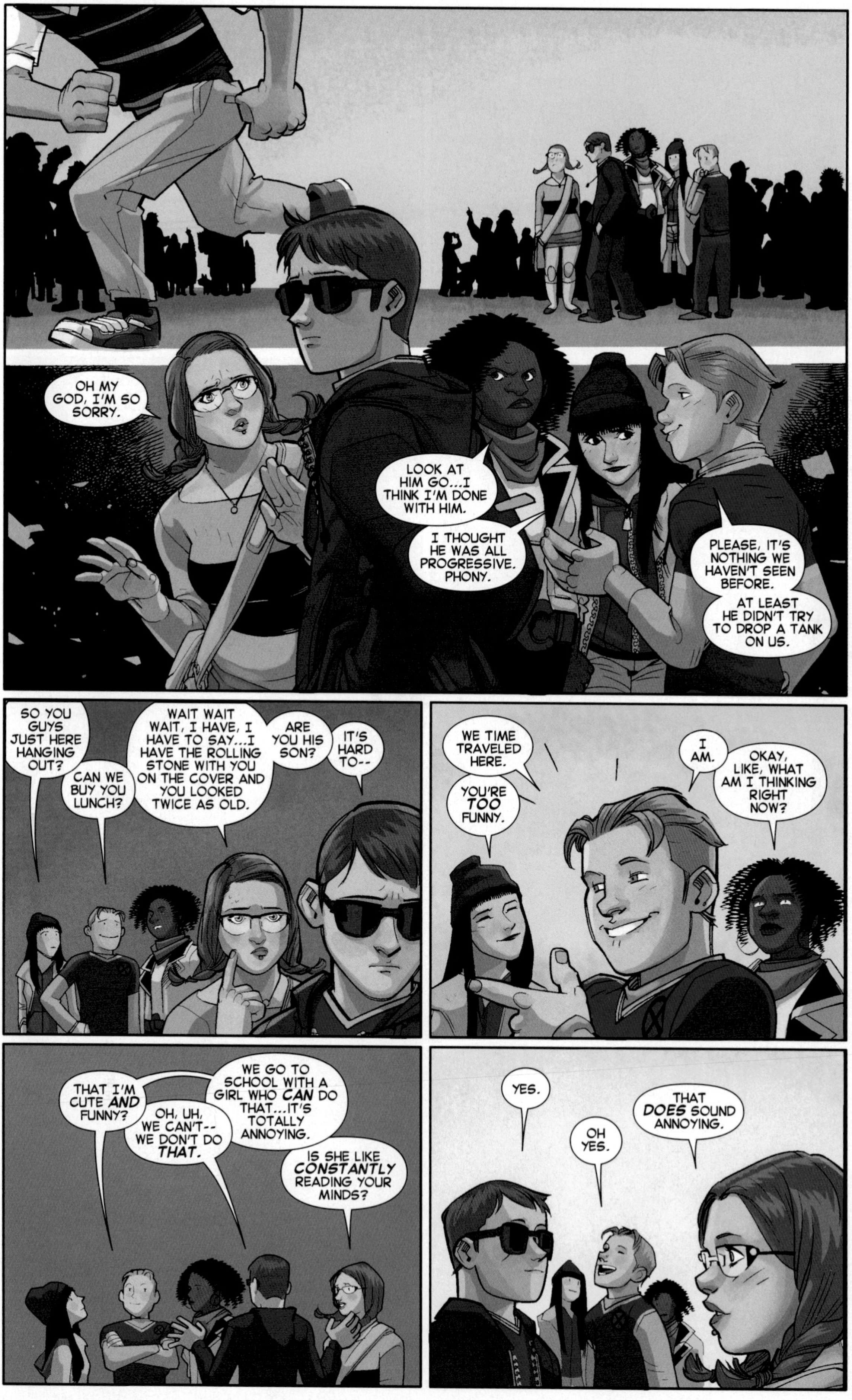

OH MY GOD, I'M SO SORRY.
LOOK AT HIM GO...I THINK I'M DONE WITH HIM.
I THOUGHT HE WAS ALL PROGRESSIVE. PHONY.
PLEASE, IT'S NOTHING WE HAVEN'T SEEN BEFORE.
AT LEAST HE DIDN'T TRY TO DROP A TANK ON US.
SO YOU GUYS JUST HERE HANGING OUT?
CAN WE BUY YOU LUNCH?
WAIT WAIT WAIT, I HAVE, I HAVE TO SAY...I HAVE THE ROLLING STONE WITH YOU ON THE COVER AND YOU LOOKED TWICE AS OLD.
ARE YOU HIS SON?
IT'S HARD TO--
WE TIME TRAVELED HERE.
YOU'RE *TOO* FUNNY.
I AM.
OKAY, LIKE, WHAT AM I THINKING RIGHT NOW?
THAT I'M CUTE *AND* FUNNY?
WE GO TO SCHOOL WITH A GIRL WHO *CAN* DO THAT...IT'S TOTALLY ANNOYING.
OH, UH, WE CAN'T-- WE DON'T DO *THAT*.
IS SHE LIKE *CONSTANTLY* READING YOUR MINDS?
YES.
OH YES.
THAT *DOES* SOUND ANNOYING.

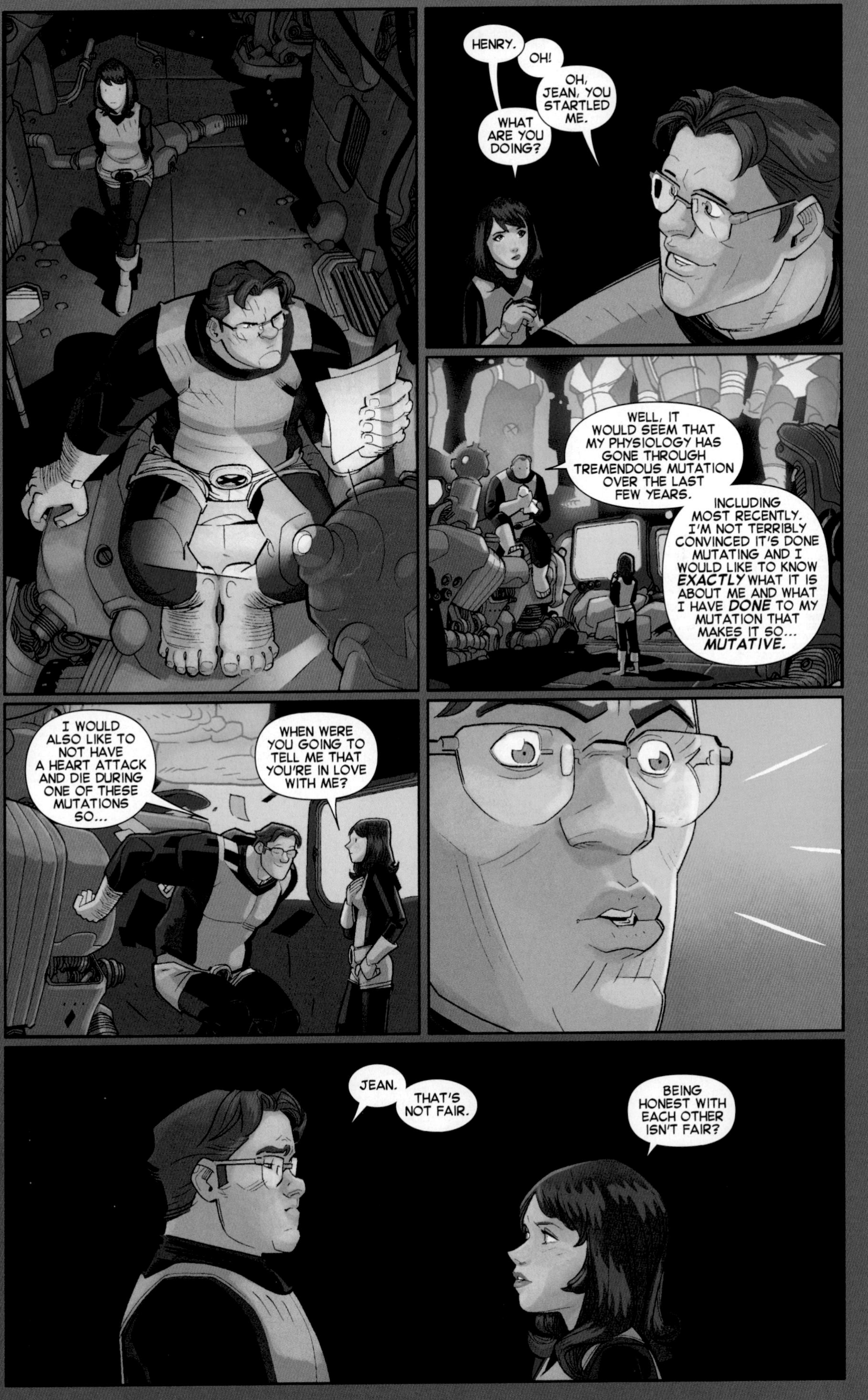
HENRY.
OH!
OH, JEAN, YOU STARTLED ME.
WHAT ARE YOU DOING?
WELL, IT WOULD SEEM THAT MY PHYSIOLOGY HAS GONE THROUGH TREMENDOUS MUTATION OVER THE LAST FEW YEARS.
INCLUDING MOST RECENTLY. I'M NOT TERRIBLY CONVINCED IT'S DONE MUTATING AND I WOULD LIKE TO KNOW EXACTLY WHAT IT IS ABOUT ME AND WHAT I HAVE DONE TO MY MUTATION THAT MAKES IT SO... MUTATIVE.
I WOULD ALSO LIKE TO NOT HAVE A HEART ATTACK AND DIE DURING ONE OF THESE MUTATIONS SO...
WHEN WERE YOU GOING TO TELL ME THAT YOU'RE IN LOVE WITH ME?
JEAN.
THAT'S NOT FAIR.
BEING HONEST WITH EACH OTHER ISN'T FAIR?

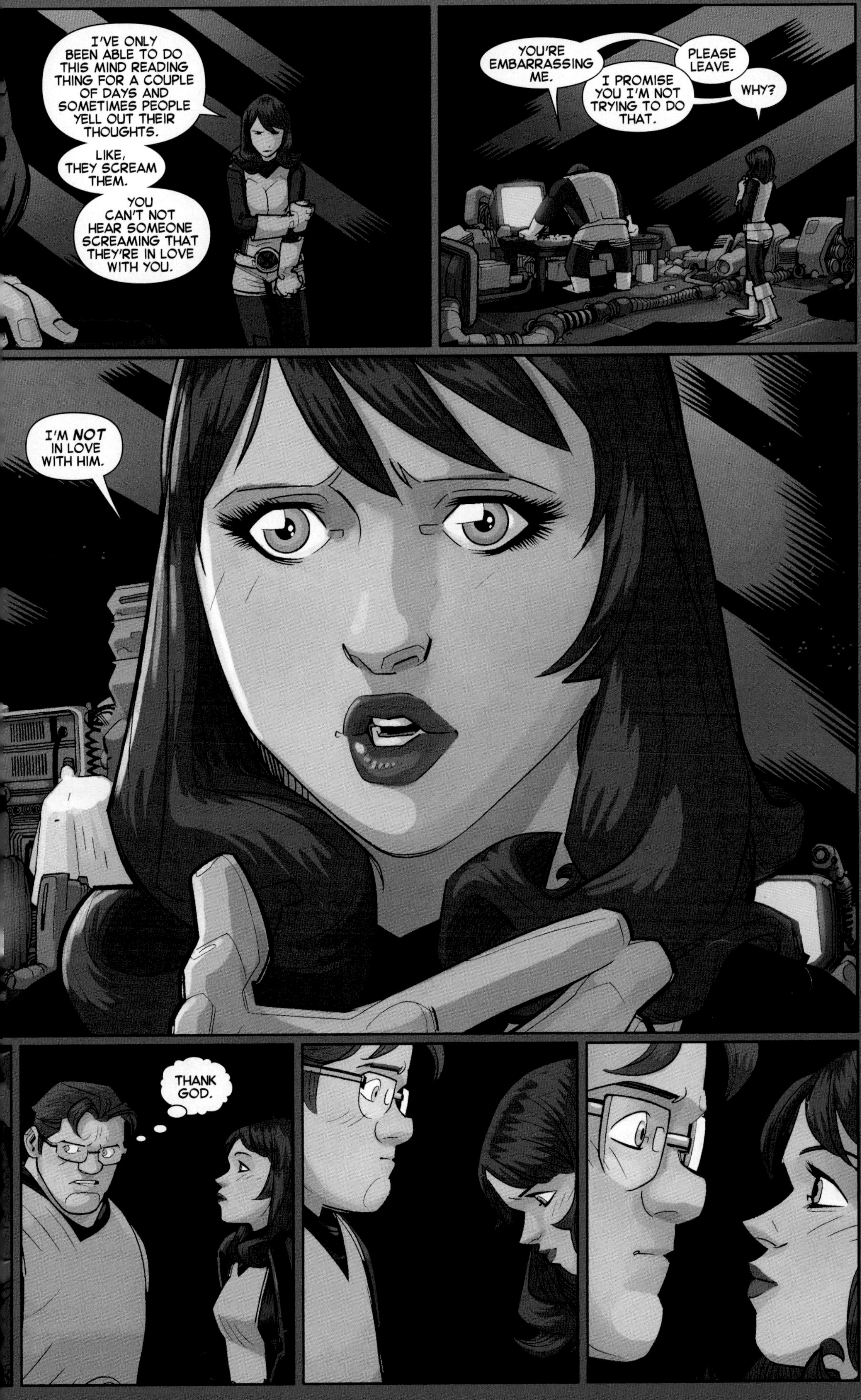
I'VE ONLY BEEN ABLE TO DO THIS MIND READING THING FOR A COUPLE OF DAYS AND SOMETIMES PEOPLE YELL OUT THEIR THOUGHTS.
LIKE, THEY SCREAM THEM.
YOU CAN'T NOT HEAR SOMEONE SCREAMING THAT THEY'RE IN LOVE WITH YOU.
YOU'RE EMBARRASSING ME.
PLEASE LEAVE.
I PROMISE YOU I'M NOT TRYING TO DO THAT.
WHY?
I'M NOT IN LOVE WITH HIM.
THANK GOD.

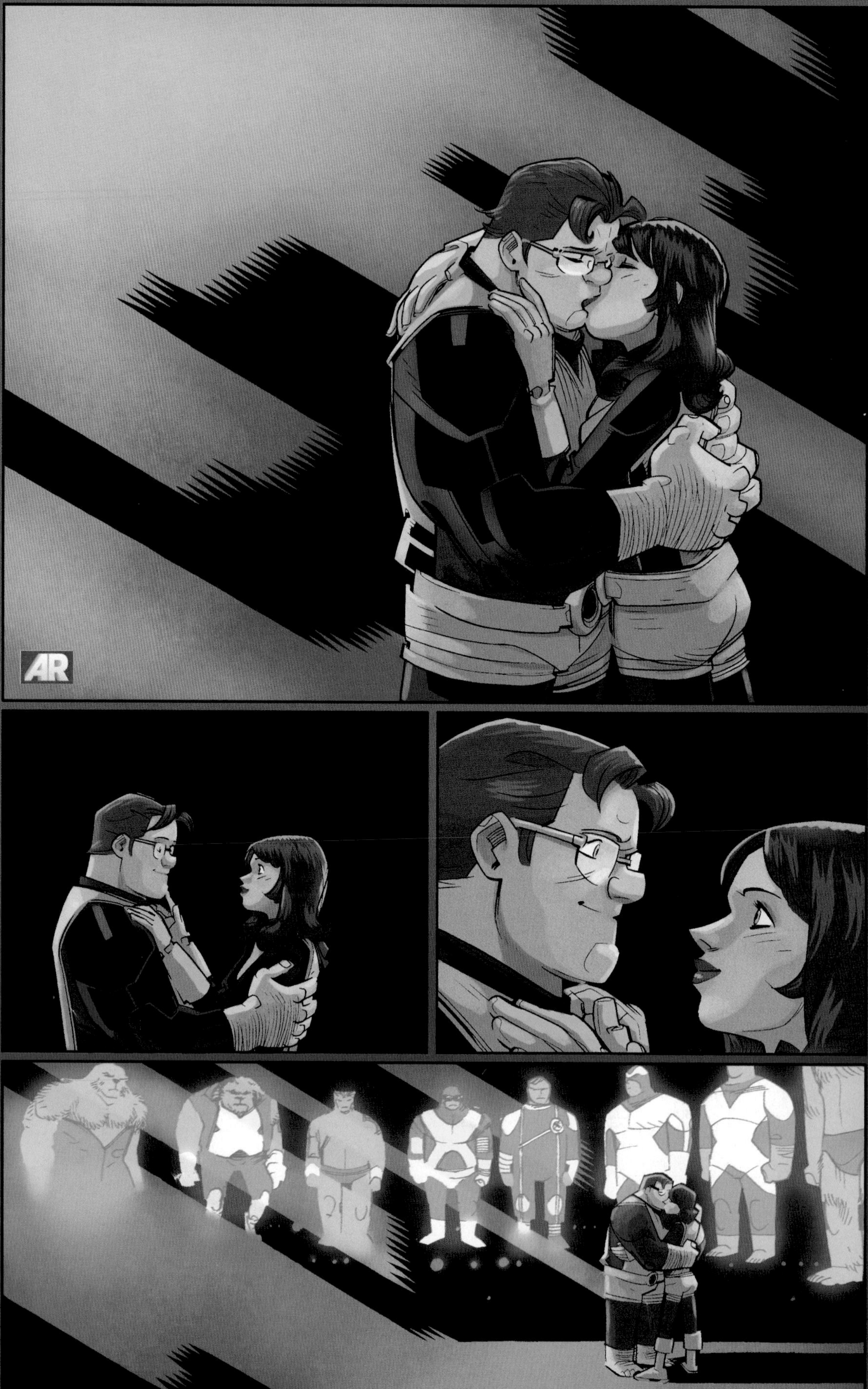

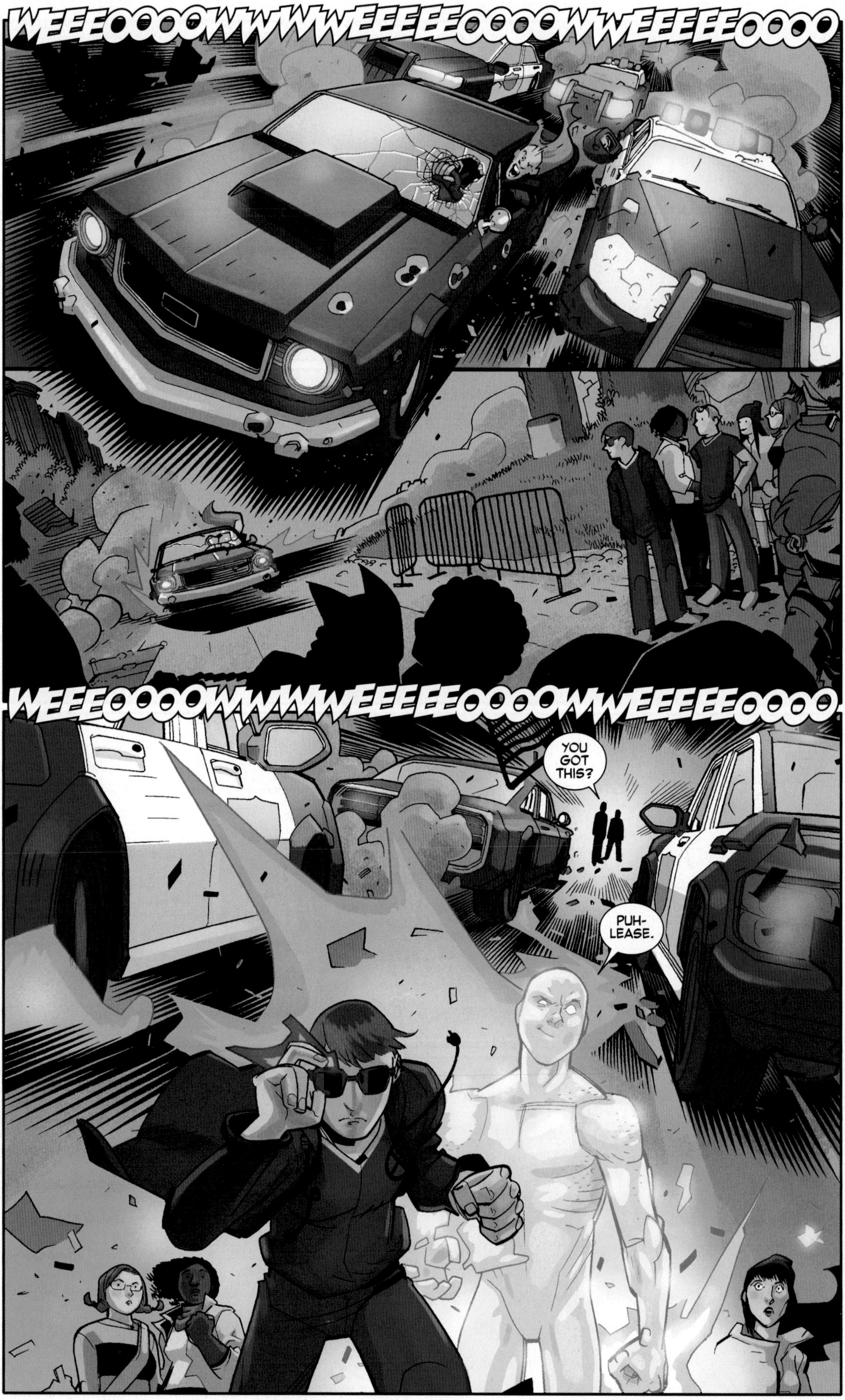

WEEEOOOOWWWWEEEEEOOOOWWEEEEEOOOO
WEEEOOOOWWWWEEEEEOOOOWWEEEEEOOOO
YOU GOT THIS?
PUH-LEASE.

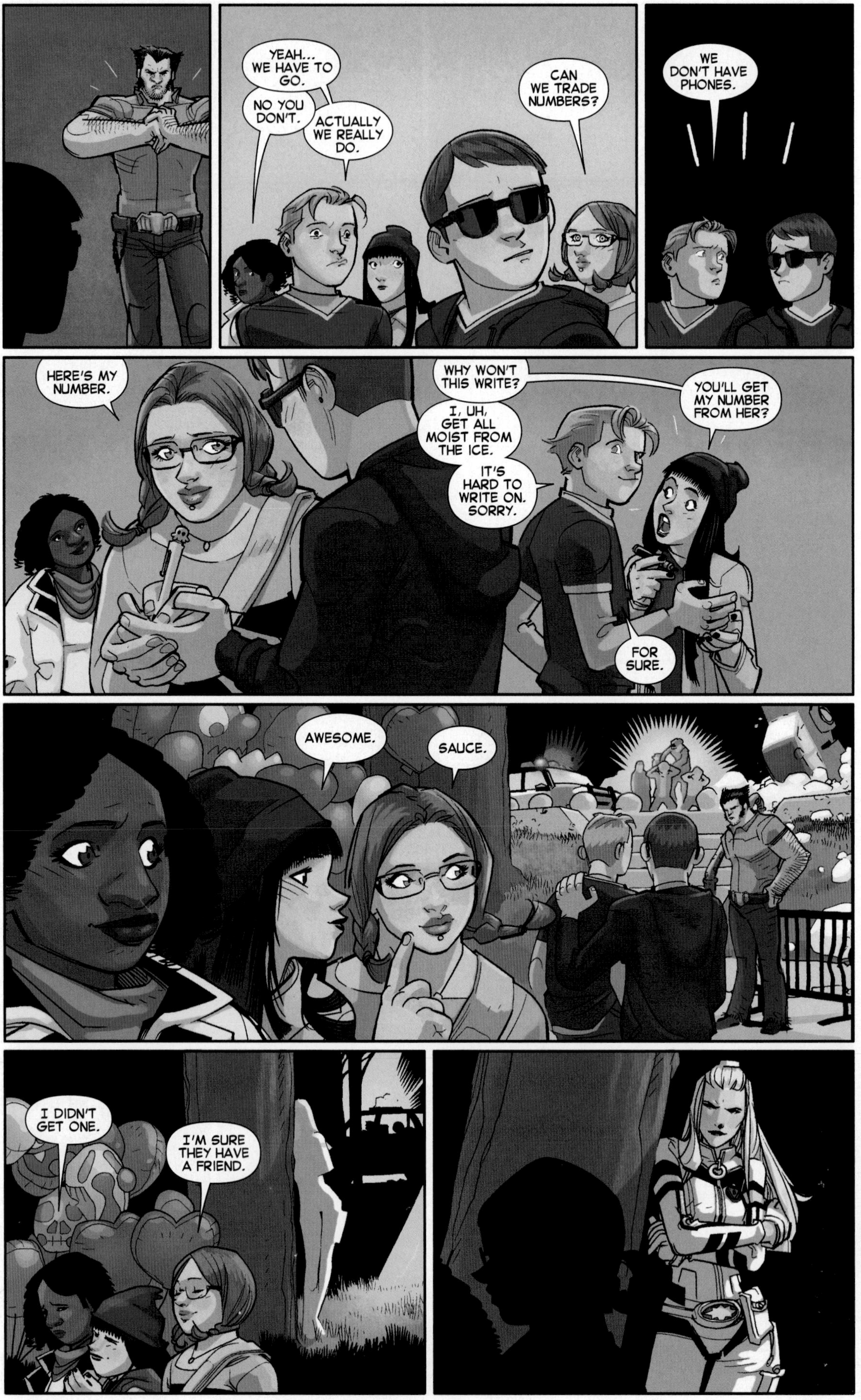
YEAH... WE HAVE TO GO.
NO YOU DON'T.
ACTUALLY WE REALLY DO.
CAN WE TRADE NUMBERS?
WE DON'T HAVE PHONES.
HERE'S MY NUMBER.
WHY WON'T THIS WRITE?
I, UH, GET ALL MOIST FROM THE ICE.
IT'S HARD TO WRITE ON. SORRY.
YOU'LL GET MY NUMBER FROM HER?
FOR SURE.
AWESOME.
SAUCE.
I DIDN'T GET ONE.
I'M SURE THEY HAVE A FRIEND.

NEXT:
BATTLE OF THE ATOM!!

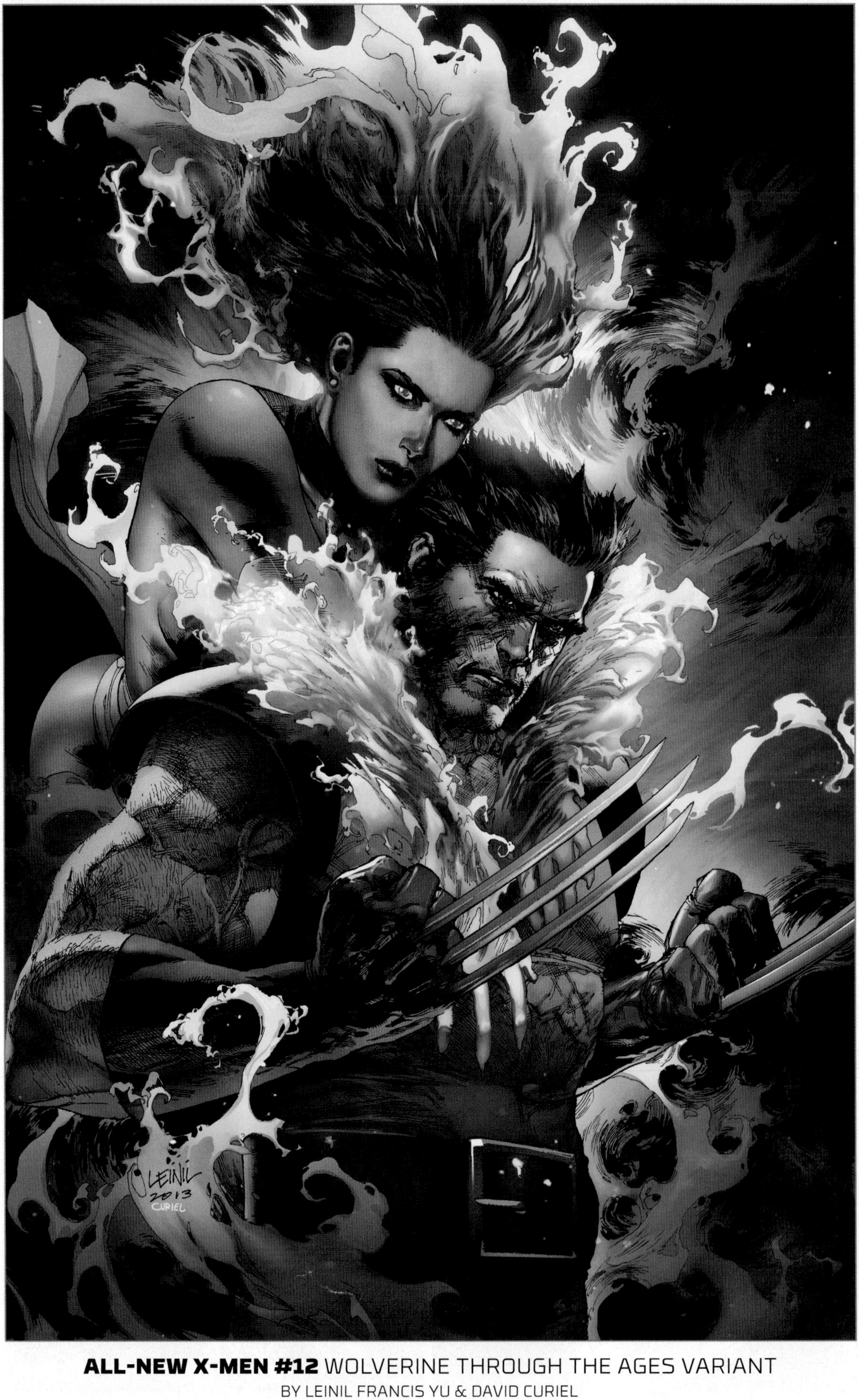
LEINIL
2013
CURIEL

ALL-NEW X-MEN #12 WOLVERINE THROUGH THE AGES VARIANT
BY LEINIL FRANCIS YU & DAVID CURIEL

#11 PENCILS

#12 SKETCHES

#13 SKETCHES

#14 SKETCHES

#14 PENCILS

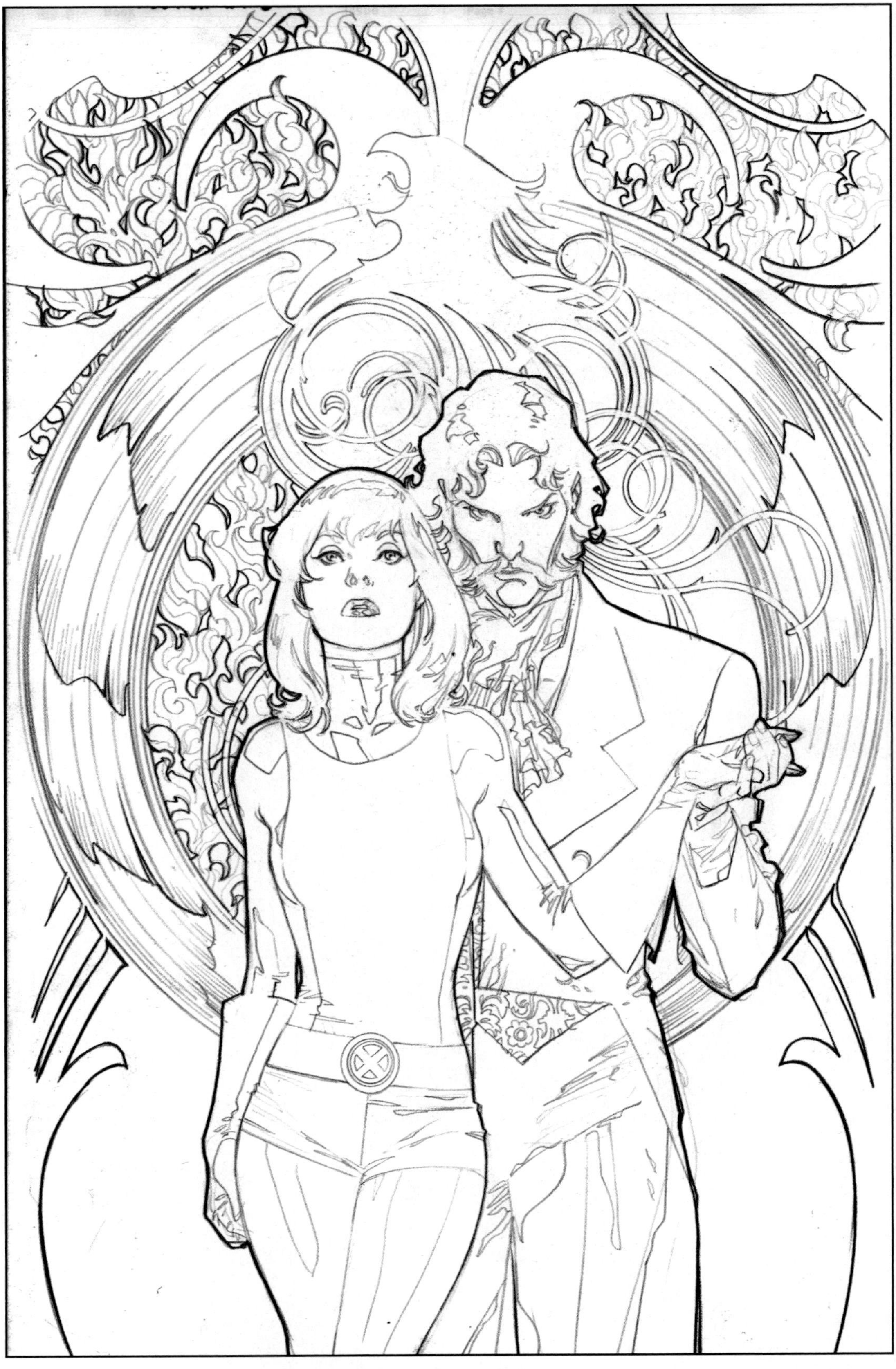

#15 SKETCHES

**#15 INKS BY
WADE VON GRAWBADGER**

#11, PAGE 4 PENCILS BY STUART IMMONEN

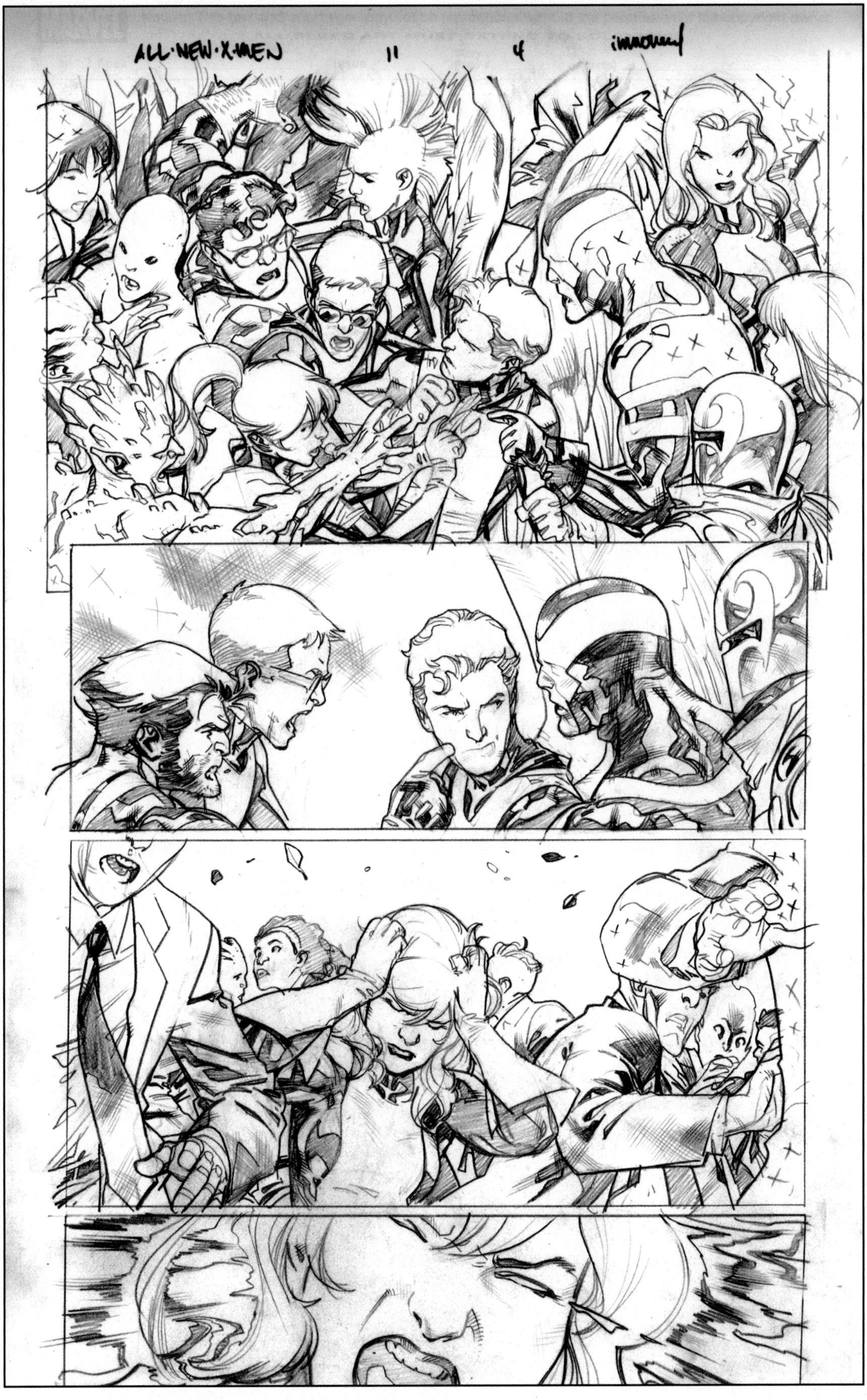
ALL·NEW·X·MEN
11
4
immonen

#12, PAGE 6 PENCILS BY STUART IMMONEN

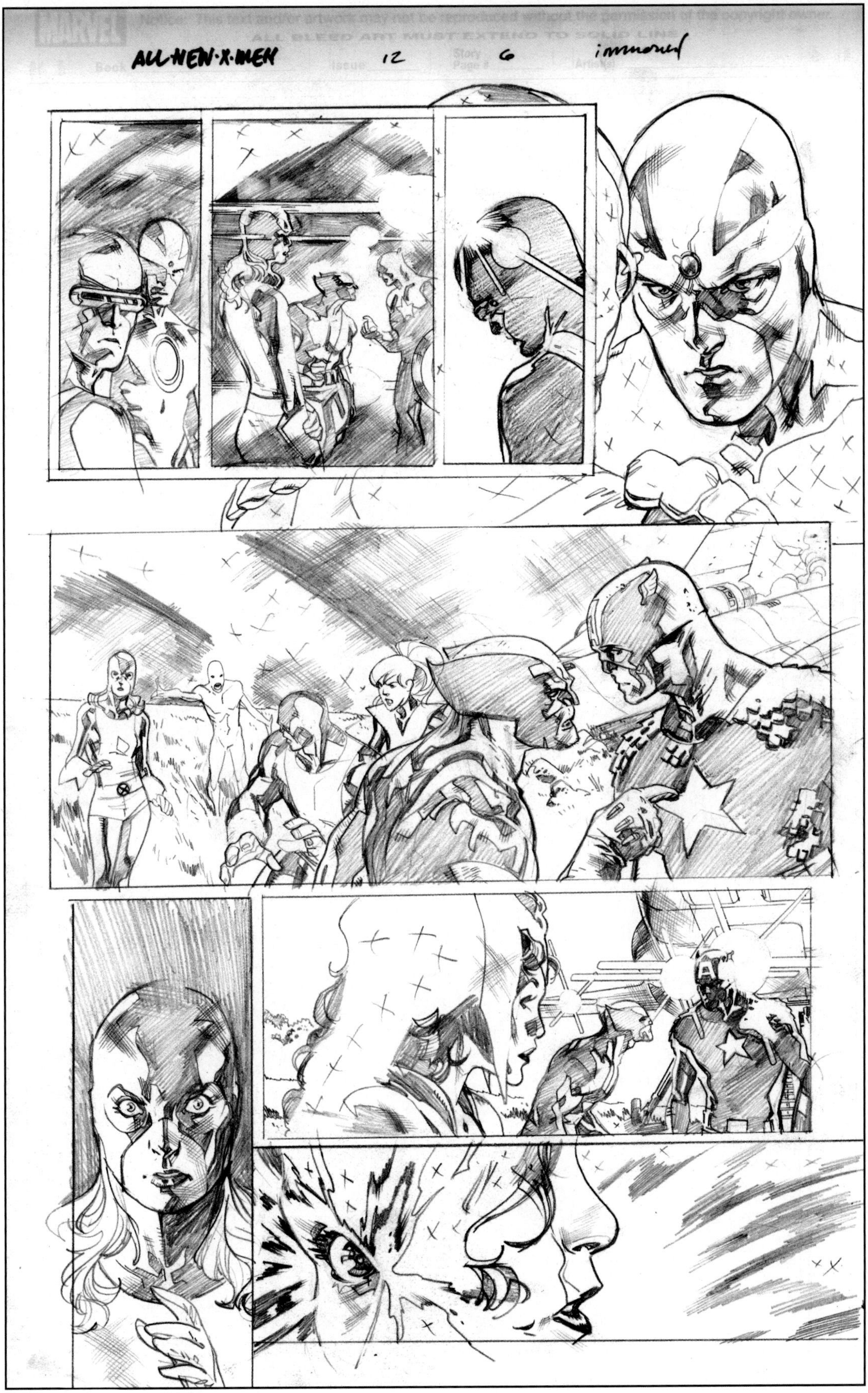
ALL BLEED ART MUST EXTEND TO SOLID LINE
Book ALL-NEW X-MEN
Issue 12
Story Page # 6
Artist(s) immonen

#13, PAGE 13 PENCILS BY STUART IMMONEN

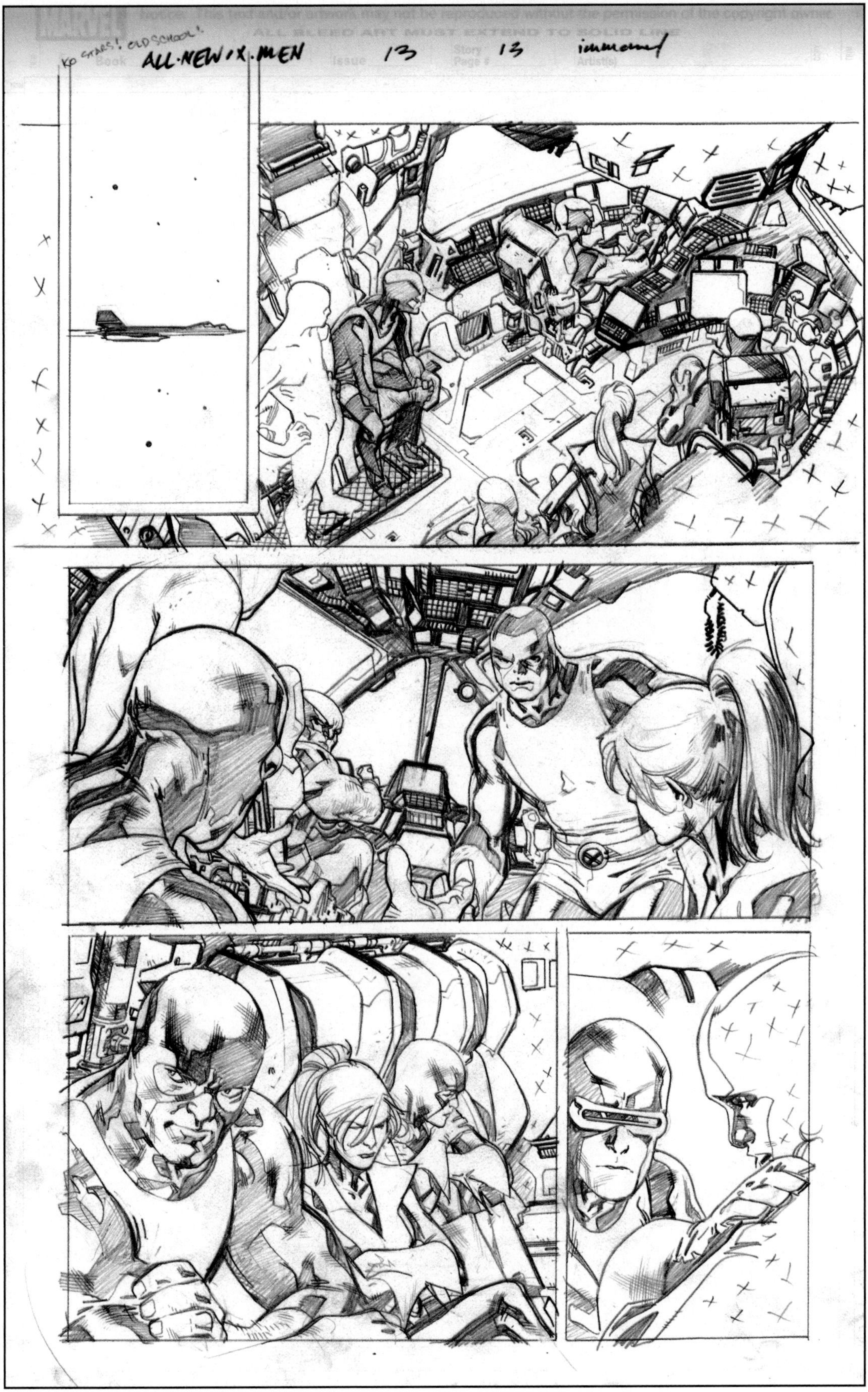
ALL BLEED ART MUST EXTEND TO SOLID LINE
KO STARS! OLD SCHOOL!
Book ALL-NEW X-MEN
Issue 13
Story Page # 13
Artist(s) immonen

#14, PAGE 6 PENCILS BY STUART IMMONEN

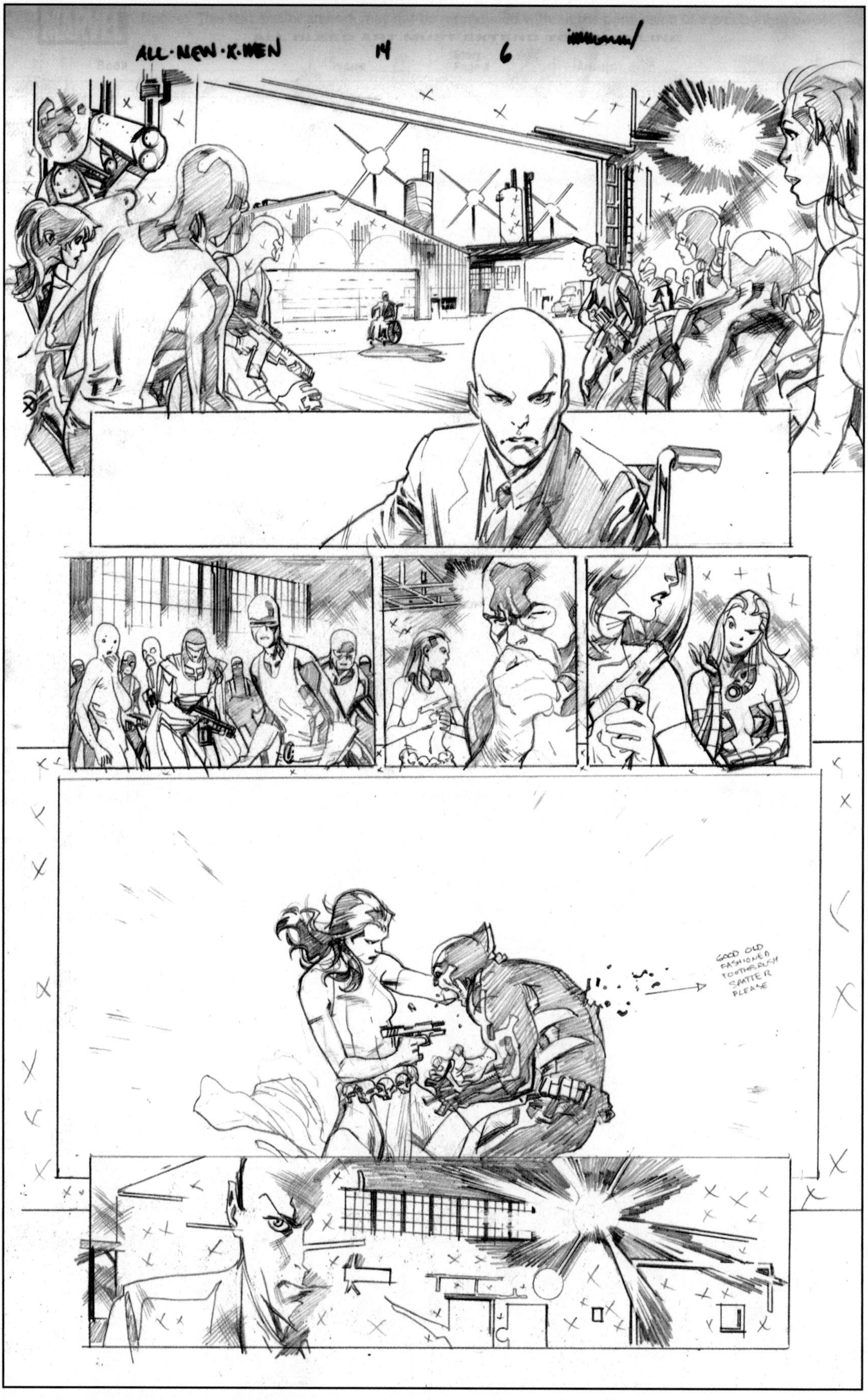
ALL·NEW·X·MEN
14
6
GOOD OLD FASHIONED TOOTHBRUSH SPATTER PLEASE

CHARACTER SKETCHES DAVID LAFUENTE

#15 LAYOUTS BY DAVID LAFUENTE

ANX #15
2
3
RG
Storm
RG
RG
RG
RG
ALL NEW XMEN #15
4
5
like
Stuart's
moar
Stew
cyclo
thinks
cyclo
ice
ice
cyclo
ice
cyclo
ice
cyclo

ANX #15
6
7
B
Beast
JG
ice
cyclo
B
JG
B
JG
wheel
ANX #15
8
9
B
ice
cyclo
CARNIVAL
ice
cyclo
ice
cyclo

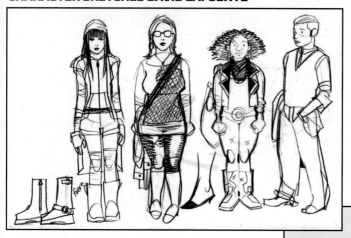

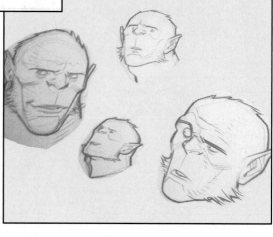

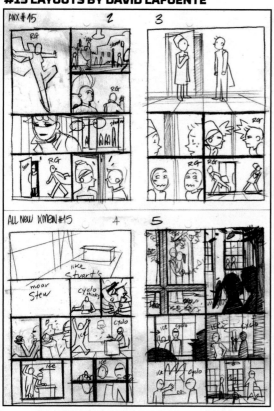

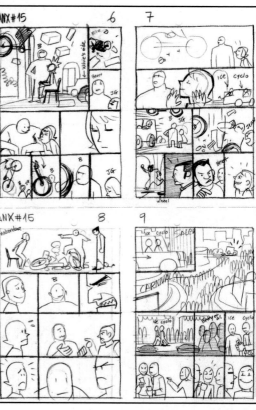

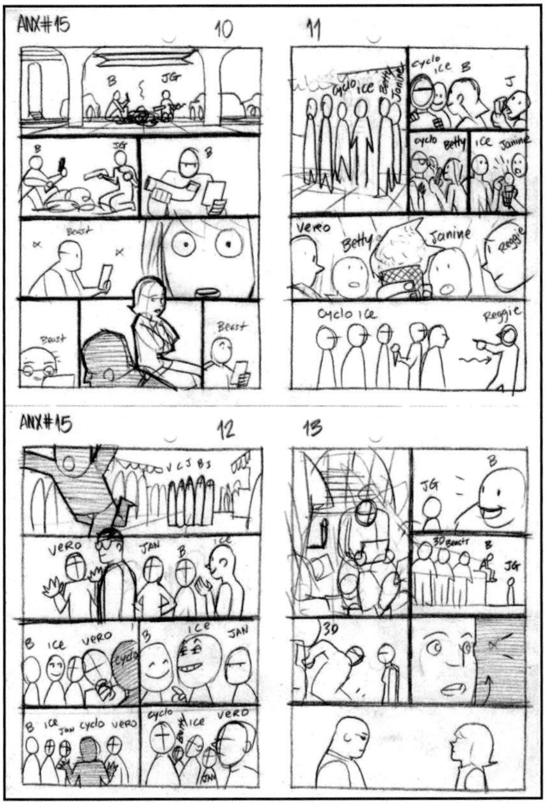
ANX#15
10
11
12
13

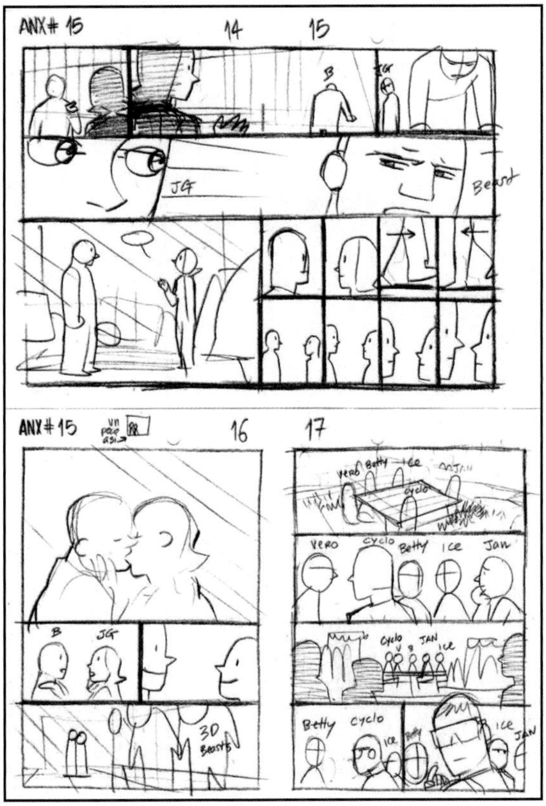
ANX#15
14
15
16
17

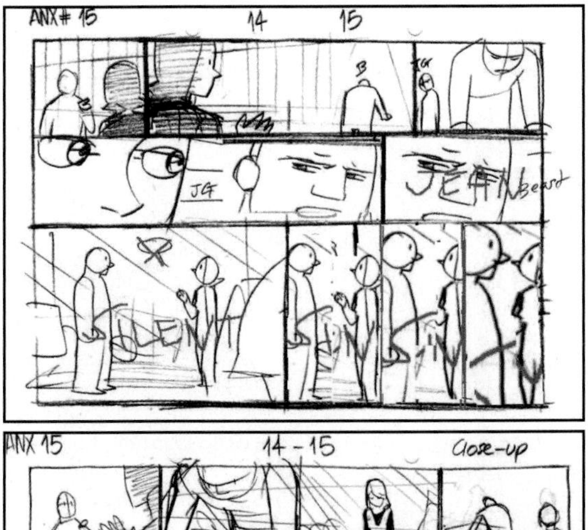
ANX#15
14
15

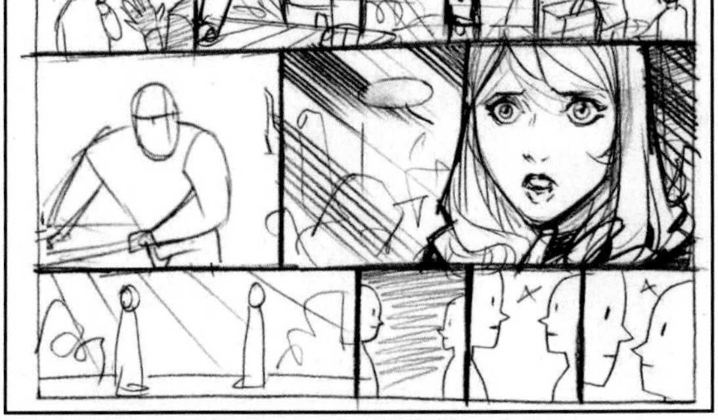
ANX 15
14 - 15
Close-up

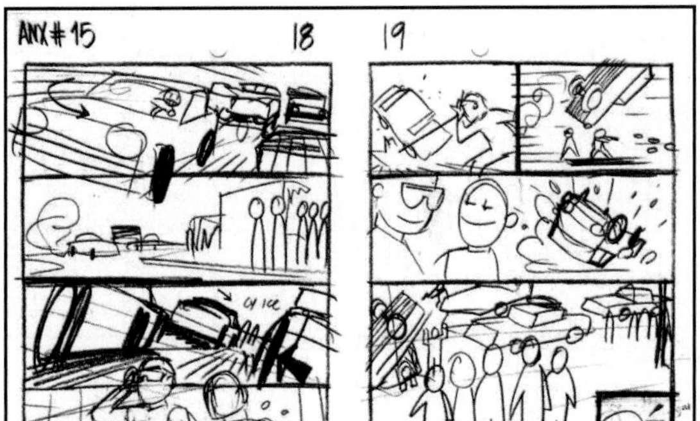
ANX#15
18
19

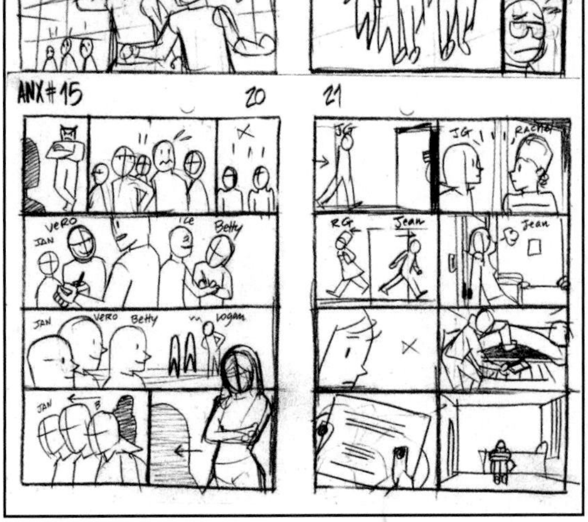
ANX#15
20
21

REVISED LAYOUTS FOR PAGES 14-15

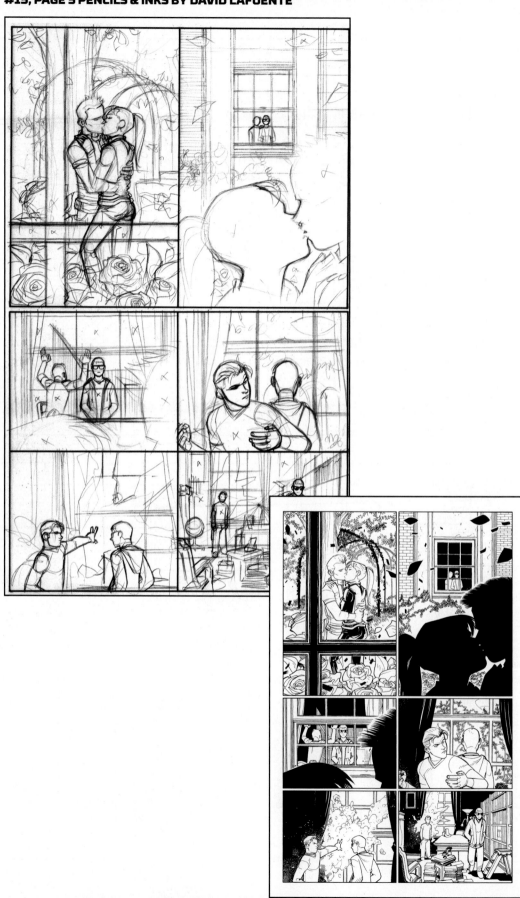

#15, PAGE 7 PENCILS & INKS BY DAVID LAFUENTE

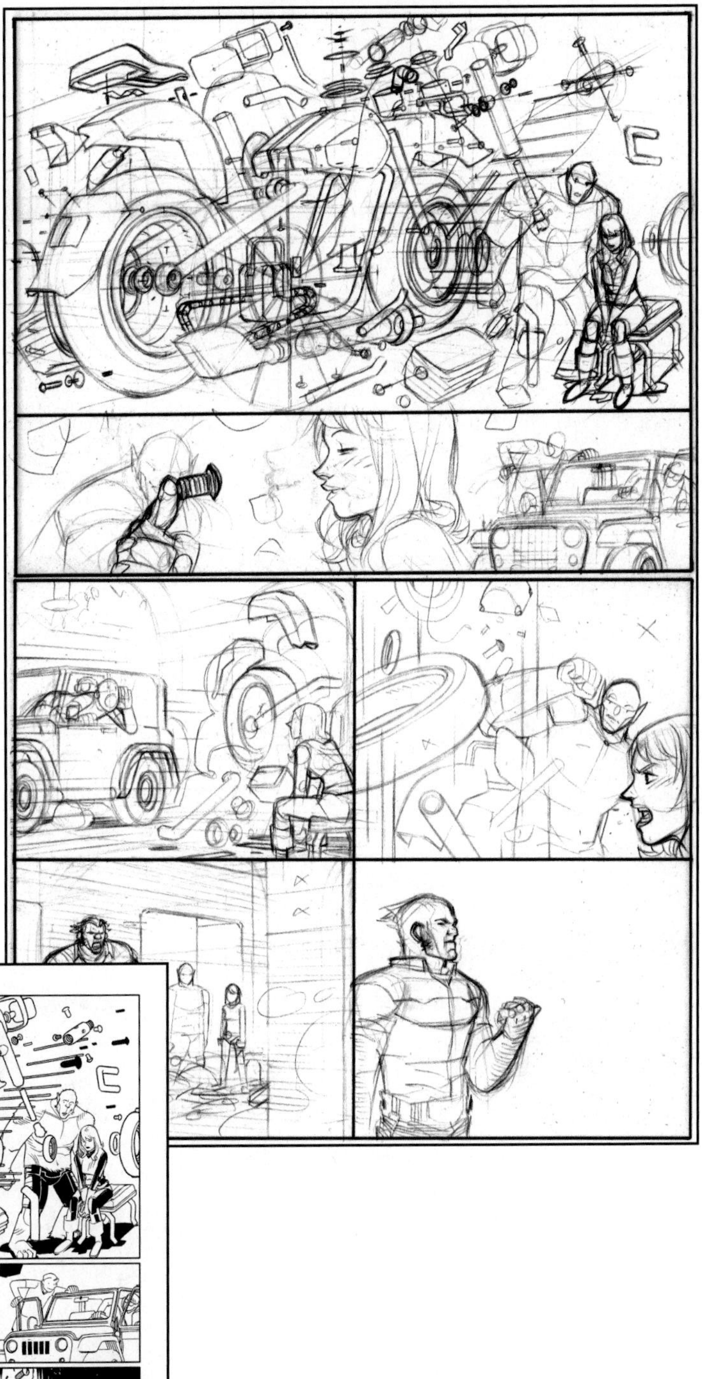

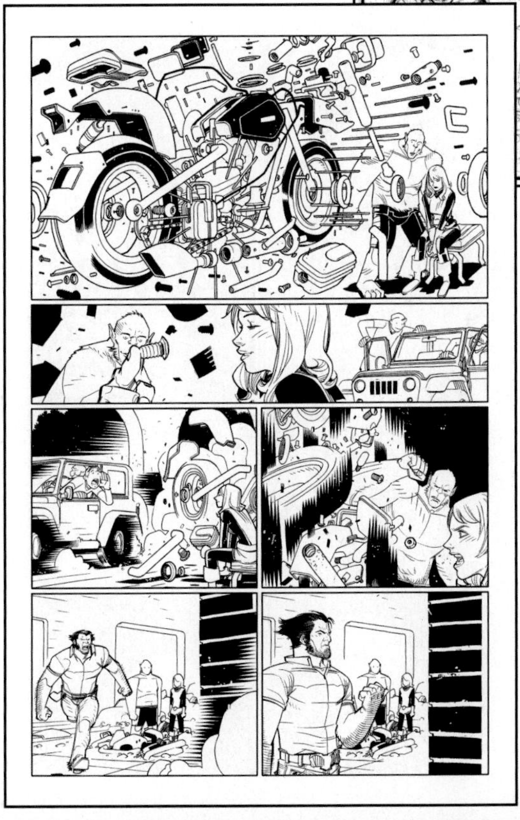

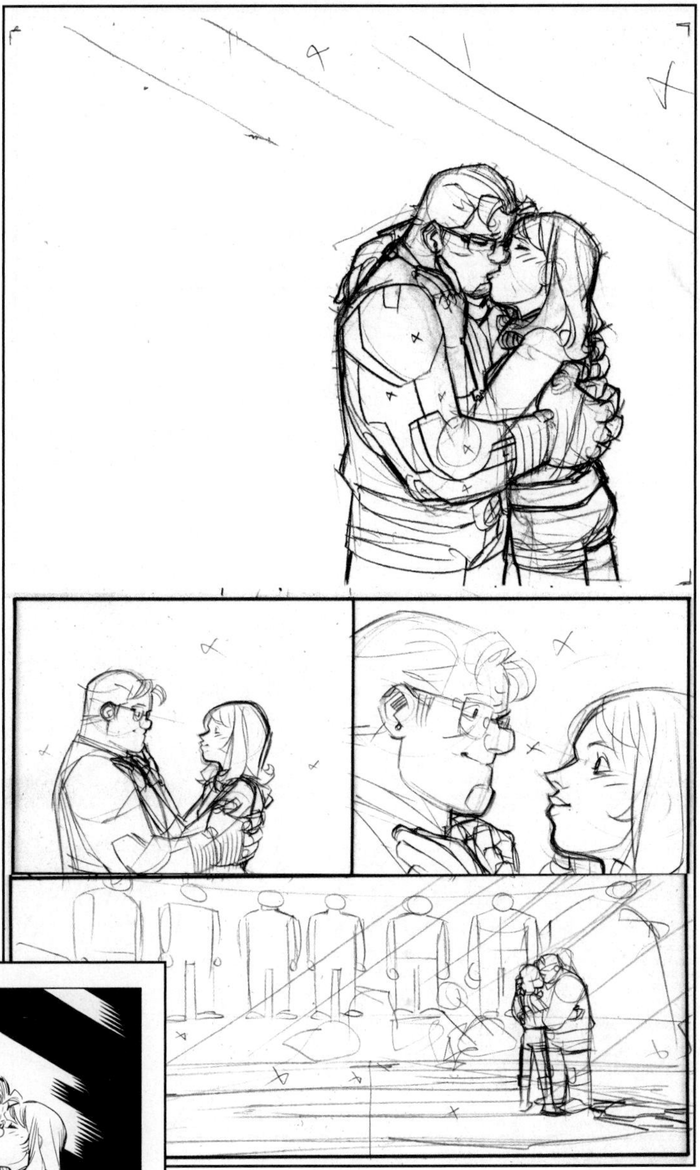

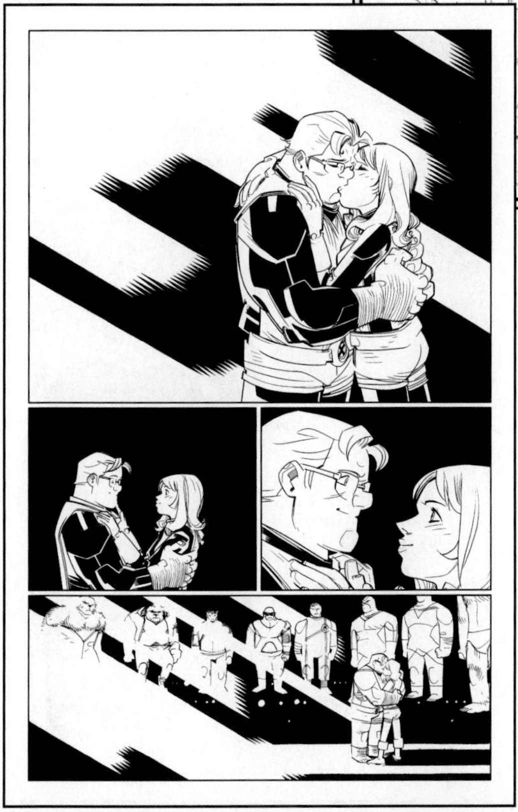

TO ACCESS THE FREE *MARVEL AUGMENTED REALITY APP* THAT ENHANCES AND CHANGES THE WAY YOU EXPERIENCE COMICS

1. **Download the app for free via** marvel.com/ARapp
2. **Launch the app on your camera-enabled Apple iOS® or Android™ device***

3. **Hold your mobile device's camera over** any cover or panel with the **AR** graph.
4. **Sit back and see the future of comics** in action!

*Available on most camera-enabled Apple iOS® and Android™ devices. Content subject to change and availability.

ALL·NEW X·MEN AR INDEX

MARVEL

TO REDEEM YOUR CODE FOR A FREE DIGITAL COPY:

1. **GO TO MARVEL.COM/REDEEM.** OFFER EXPIRES ON 9/18/15.
2. **FOLLOW THE ON-SCREEN INSTRUCTIONS** TO REDEEM YOUR DIGITAL COPY.
3. **LAUNCH THE MARVEL COMICS APP TO** READ YOUR COMIC NOW!
4. **YOUR DIGITAL COPY WILL BE FOUND** UNDER THE *MY COMICS* TAB.
5. **READ & ENJOY!**

YOUR FREE DIGITAL COPY WILL BE AVAILABLE ON:

MARVEL COMICS APP FOR APPLE® iOS DEVICES	MARVEL COMICS APP FOR ANDROID™ DEVICES